Planet Earth

William Merrick, Joan O'Sullivan, Frances Stratton

• The dynamic Earth • Rocks and fossils • Water and stone •
• The Earth and its climate • The solar system • Four case studies •

Oxford University Press 1993

Oxford University Press, Walton Street, Oxford OX2 6DP

Oxford New York Toronto Delhi Bombay Calcutta Madras Karachi
Kuala Lumpur Singapore Hong Kong Tokyo Nairobi Dar es Salaam
Cape Town Melbourne Auckland Madrid
and associated companies in
Berlin Ibadan

Oxford is a trade mark of Oxford University Press

© William Merrick, Joan O'Sullivan, Frances Stratton
All rights reserved. No part of this publication may be reproduced, stored in a retrieval system, or transmitted, in any form or by any means, without the prior permission in writing of Oxford University Press. Within the U.K., exceptions are allowed in respect of any fair dealing for the purpose of research or private study, or criticism or review, as permitted under the Copyright, Designs and Patents Act, 1988, or in the case of reprographic reproduction in accordance with the terms of licences issued by the Copyright Licensing Agency. Enquiries concerning reproduction outside these terms and in other countries should be sent to the Rights Department, Oxford University Press, at the address above.

ISBN 0 19 914364 1

Typeset in $10\frac{1}{2}/14$ pt Monotype Joanna and Bell Gothic by
MS Filmsetting Ltd, Frome, Somerset

First published 1993

Printed in Hong Kong

A CIP catalogue record for this book is available from the British Library

Coordinating Editors: David Appleby, Alan Jarvis, William Merrick, Joan O'Sullivan

Photographs
The publishers wish to thank the following for permission to reproduce transparencies:
J. Allan Cash pp17, 21 (T.L. and B.L.); **Bruce Coleman** p46; **Mary Evans Picture Library** p52; **Geoscience** p9; **GSF Picture Library** p10; **Robert Harding** p50; **The Mansell Collection** p5 (T.R.); **The Met. Office** p35; **NASA** pp38, 41, 53; **Natural History Museum** p15; **Novosti Press** p25; **Ann Ronan** p48 (T); **The Science Photo Library** pp5 (B.L.), 8, 20, 21 (R), 32, 33, 36, 37 (T.R. and B.R.), 39 (B), 42 (T), 47, 48 (B), 49, 55; **The Telegraph Colour Library** pp6, 37 (L), 39 (T); **Thearle Photography** p44; **TRH/NASA** p42 (B); **Tony Waltham** pp5 (T.L.), 12, 13, 16 (T and B), 23, 24; **Zefa** p16 (M).

Illustrations are by:
Isabell Bowring (c/o Temple Rogers) p18; **Julie Chapman** p23; **Michael Eaton** pp4, 7 (B), 8, 9, 46 (T); **Martina Farrow** pp27, 34, 35 (T), 52 (T); **Sarah Govia** p29; **Oxford Illustrators** p54; **Chris Price** pp19, 43; **Adam Stower** p45 (L); **Michael Worthington** pp28, 30-33, 36, 40 (B), 49-52, 55; **Galina Zolfaghari** pp6, 7 (T), 14, 15 (T), 17, 18, 22, 24-26, 38, 39, 41, 44-46.

How to use this book

This book is not intended to be read consecutively from beginning to end. It is designed to give you more active involvement in how to learn science.

The book is made up of six sections. Each section contains four different types of page which you should use in different ways:

✷ Visual stimulus
These highly illustrated pages are designed to bring you into the topic in an interesting way and get you thinking. Use the *Factfile* and other resources to help you with the activities.

ⓘ Factfile
These pages bring together essential information about the topic of the section. You should dip into the *Factfile* as and when you need to and use it to help you to answer the questions in the rest of the section. The *Key facts* box summarizes the main points you should have learnt from the section. The *Factfile* is also helpful for revision.

📖 Background reading
This contains one or two articles to give you an understanding of how the science you are learning fits into the outside world. These often deal with topical and contentious issues. It is important that you should grasp the underlying science in such issues so that you can make an informed judgement. Use the activities at the end to test your understanding.

？ Questions and activities
As you answer the questions on these pages, you will be taken through the facts and ideas covered in the section, helping you to learn them. There are various kinds of activities and your teacher will help you to choose the right ones for you.

✚ Extension pages
These can be found at the end of the book. They allow you to practice the important skill of making sense of information in the form of words, graphs or tables and using this data to answer questions.

Contents

The dynamic Earth
- ✷ Inside the planet   4
- ✷ The dynamic Earth   5
- ⓘ Factfile   6
- 📖 Shaping the crust   8
- ？ Questions and activities   10

Rocks and fossils
- ✷ Cliff peril   12
- ✷ Rocks   13
- ⓘ Factfile   14
- 📖 History in the rocks   16
- ？ Questions and activities   18

Water and stone
- ✷ Water, water everywhere   20
- ✷ Quarries – assets or liabilities?   21
- ⓘ Factfile   22
- 📖 Leaking rocks   24
- 📖 A new dead sea   25
- ？ Questions and activities   26

The Earth and its climate
- ✷ The spinning Earth   28
- ✷ Seasonal changes   29
- ⓘ Factfile   30
- 📖 From breezes to hurricanes   32
- ？ Questions and activities   34

The solar system
- ✷ Eclipse   36
- ✷ Mars   37
- ⓘ Factfile   38
- 📖 Pulling together   40
- ？ Questions and activities   42

Case studies
- 📖 A folded landscape   44
- 📖 Eruption   46
- 📖 The dynamic Universe   48
- 📖 Japan: a disaster waiting to happen   50

Extension pages
- ✚ Bode's rule   52
- ✚ The night sky   54

Index   56

The dynamic Earth

Inside the planet

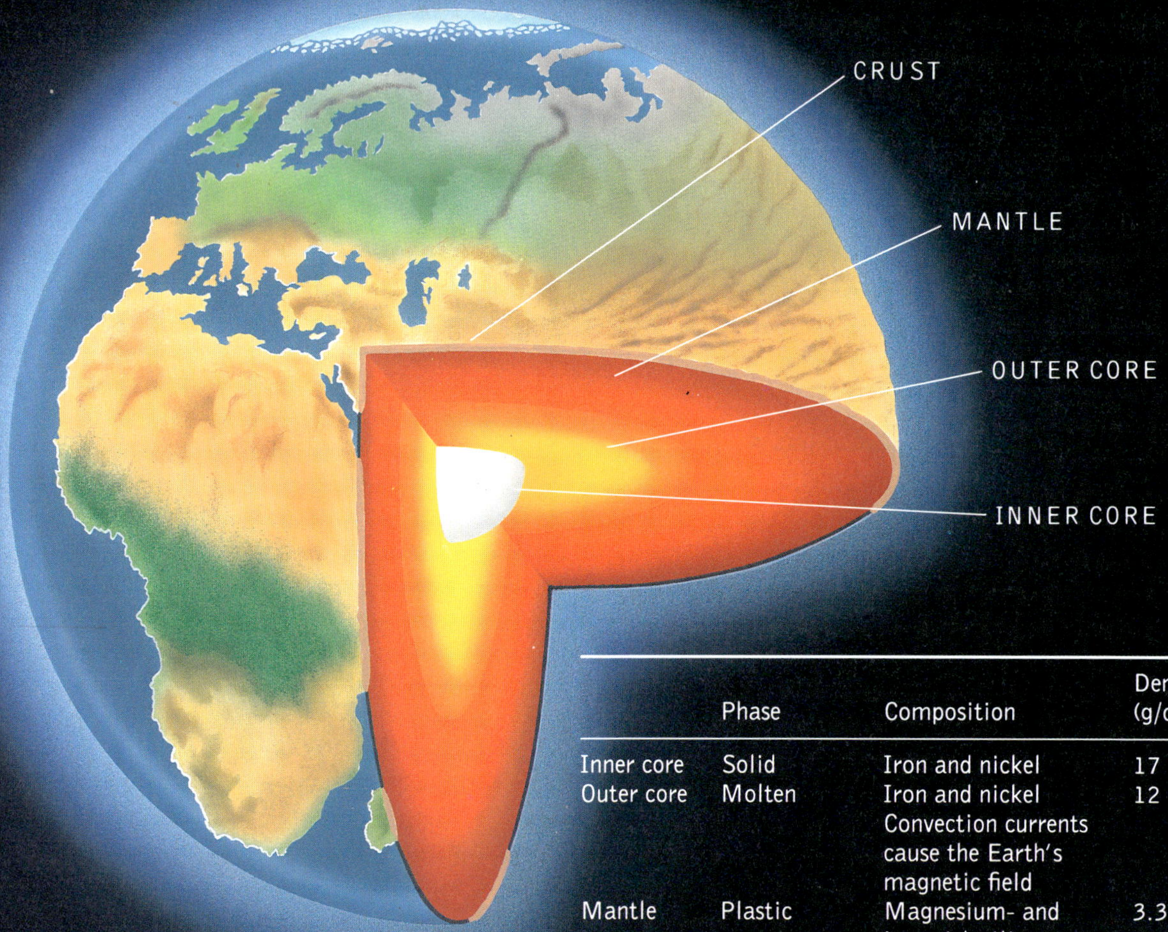

	Phase	Composition	Density (g/cm³)
Inner core	Solid	Iron and nickel	17
Outer core	Molten	Iron and nickel Convection currents cause the Earth's magnetic field	12
Mantle	Plastic	Magnesium- and iron-rich silicates	3.3
Crust	Solid	Rock	2.9

A *Journey to the Centre of the Earth.* In 1864, Jules Verne wrote a story about a group of adventurers who went deep into the Earth, where they found huge caverns inhabited by prehistoric creatures.

Imagine trying to take a *real* journey to the centre of the Earth. You would need to drill a hole nearly 6400 km deep! What changes would you find as you drilled down?

B Nobody has ever really seen what it is like deep inside the Earth: the deepest hole ever drilled is in the USSR, and that is only 13 km deep. But there are other kinds of evidence which tell us what the interior of the Earth is like without actually having to go inside. Discuss this in class, and follow it up with a library visit. Write down one piece of evidence for each of these statements:
a The Earth has a thin crust of solid rock; below that is a layer of hot plastic rock called **magma**.
b The temperature increases as we go nearer to the centre.
c The pressure increases as we go deeper.
d The core of the Earth is made of iron and nickel.

Visual stimulus

The dynamic Earth

The dynamic Earth

The surface of the Earth is always changing. Earthquakes and volcanoes continually disturb the surface, and over long periods of time the surface becomes folded and cracked. New mountains are formed and old ones wear away, and even the shape and position of the continents slowly change.

Earthquake. In 1755 the city of Lisbon was destroyed by a massive earthquake.

Volcano. Molten rock escapes from inside the planet. 'Diamond pipe' volcanoes bring up rocks from 250 km below the surface.

▲ **Folding.** These layers of rock were once horizontal.

◄ **Faulting.** The surface has cracked and the two sides have moved, causing earthquakes.

A Make a time line for your classroom wall and enter in it all the volcanic eruptions you can find out about. Is there any sign that the world's volcanic activity is calming down?

B Folding of rocks can be on an enormous scale. Mountain ranges can be formed as the crust buckles. Use the school library to find out when and where fold mountain ranges were formed in Britain.

Visual stimulus 5

The dynamic Earth

Key facts: the dynamic Earth

- The Earth is composed of a thin, solid **crust** floating on a **mantle** made of hot plastic rock or magma, a molten metallic **outer core** and small, solid, metallic **inner core**. The inner layers are under great pressure.

- **Magma** is a hot, plastic fluid formed in the crust and upper mantle. When it escapes from volcanoes it is called **lava**.

- The rocky crust is made up of **tectonic plates** which float on the mantle and move very slowly against each other, causing **continental drift**.

- Once the continental plates were all together forming one supercontinent. Since then, over millions of years they have drifted apart.

- Volcanoes and earthquakes occur where plates are moving together, scraping alongside or moving away from each other. Fold mountain ranges are also built where plates collide.

Tectonic plates: a planet-sized jigsaw

The Earth's crust is broken into a small number of rigid 'plates', which float on the plastic rock (magma) of the mantle. Convection currents in the magma cause the plates to move. On average, they move about 20 mm/year. In some places, plates are colliding, in others they are moving apart. This movement causes **continental drift**.

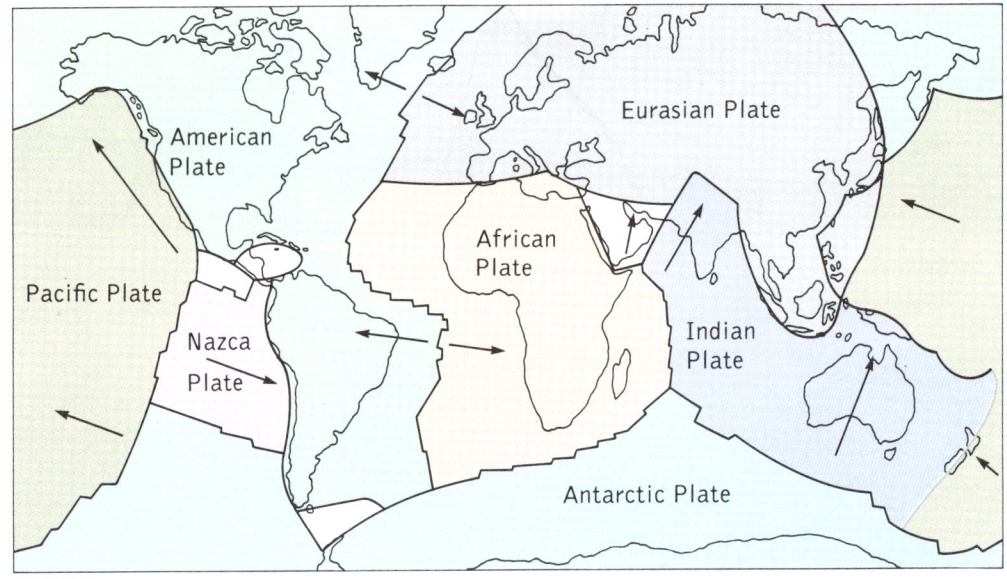

▲ The major tectonic plates.   ▼ A satellite image of the Earth, showing the oceanic ridges.

Continental drift

The magma of the mantle is a thick ('viscous') material which flows slowly, rather like pitch, carrying the plates with it. About 600 million years ago all the continents were joined together in one huge land mass, named **Pangaea** ('all lands'). Since then, continental drift has caused the crustal plates to separate. Today, we can still see how the continents would fit together. The types of rock still match where two continents were once joined, even though they may now be thousands of kilometres apart. The wildlife too shows links: marsupials such as opossums are found mainly in Australia, but opossums also live in South America.

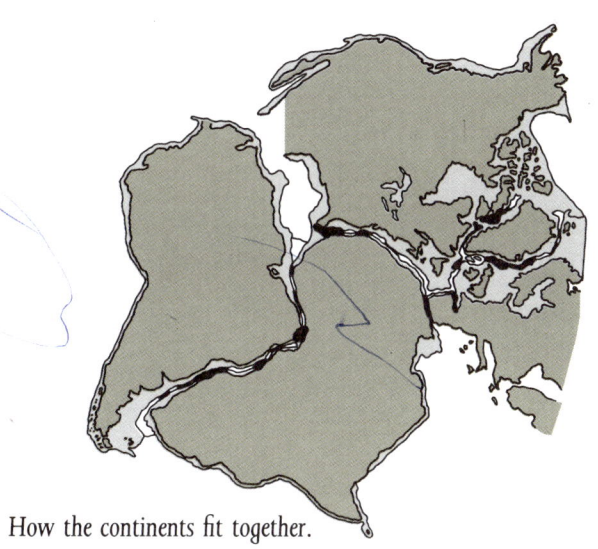

How the continents fit together.

Where are volcanoes and earthquake zones found?

Earthquake zones and volcanoes form clear patterns across the Earth's surface. They are mostly found in zones along the edges of tectonic plates. Where plate boundaries occur under the oceans, chains of volcanoes are found on the sea floor.

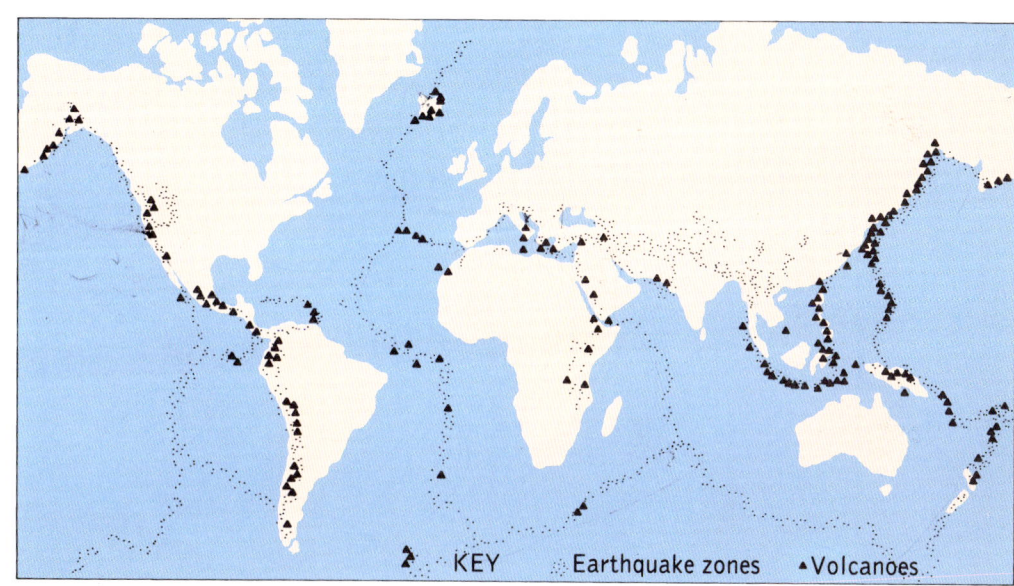

Most earthquake zones and volcanic areas are found at the edges of tectonic plates.

Plates moving together

Where plates collide, one plate is pushed under the other and melts back into the mantle. In most cases an ocean plate collides with and slides under a continental plate. Such **convergence zones** produce deep **ocean trenches**, with linked **volcanic island arcs**, such as Japan. The plate movement causes strong earthquakes. Massive folding and faulting at the collision point can also build mountain ranges.

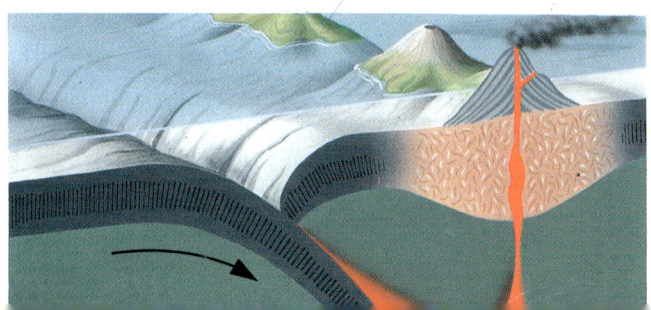

Plates moving apart

Where plates move apart, magma comes out of the mantle and cools down to form new rock. Such **divergence zones** usually arise in the oceans and are marked by the **mid-oceanic ridges**. The Earth's crust is cracked along the ridges. Volcanoes occur along the ridges and the movement of the plates causes earthquakes.

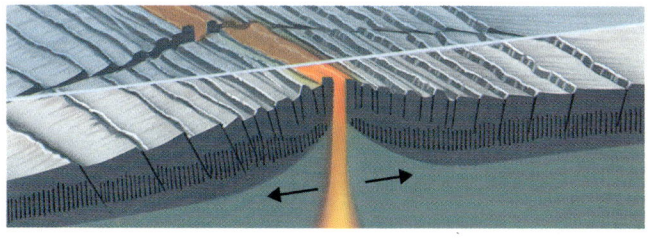

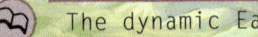 The dynamic Earth

Shaping the crust

There are two types of plate:

Oceanic plate. This underlies the oceans. It is relatively thin – about 8 km thick – and is made of basalt.

Continental plate. This carries the continents. It is thicker than oceanic plate – about 35 km thick – and is made of granite, and sedimentary and metamorphic rocks. It is less dense than oceanic plate.

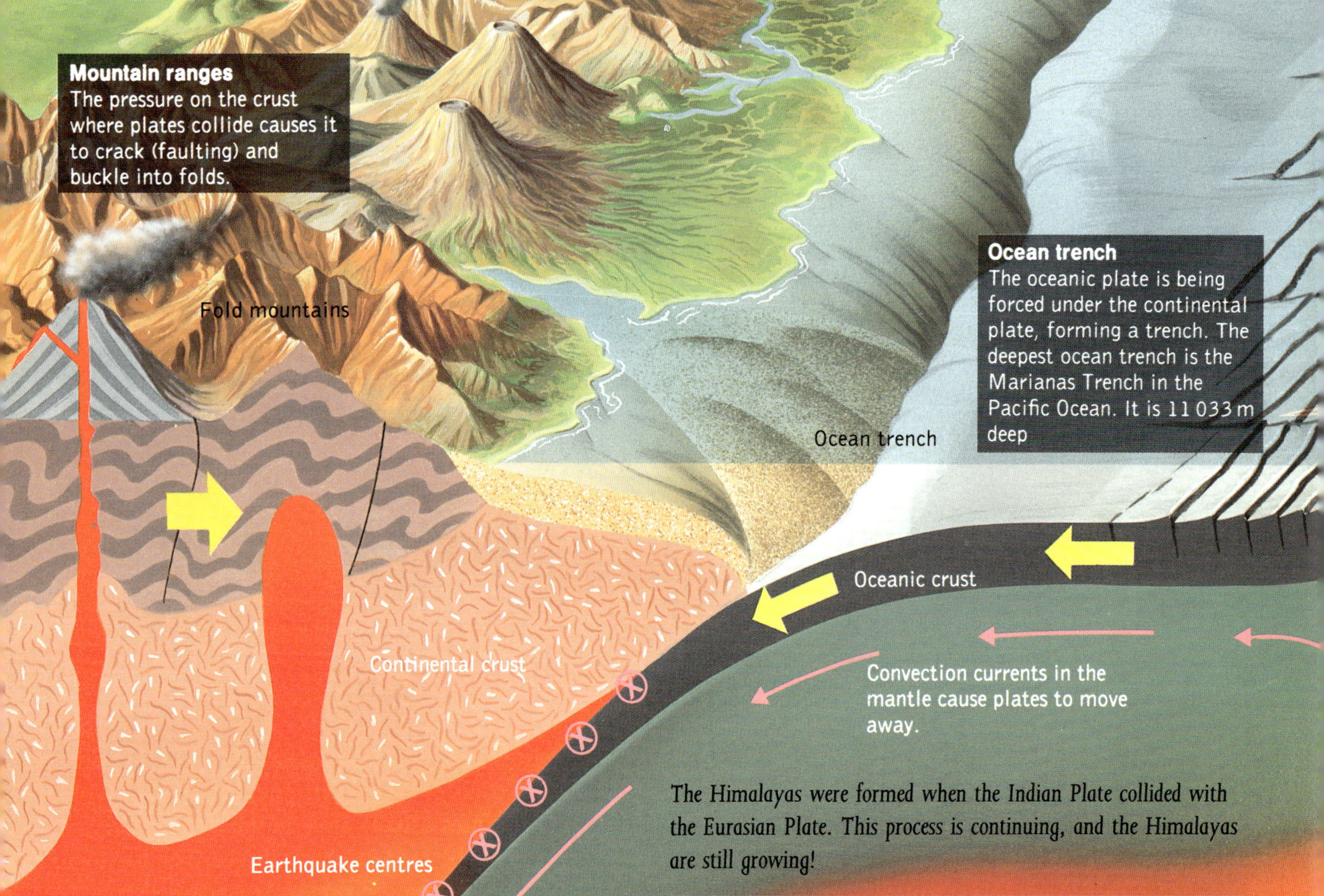

Mountain ranges
The pressure on the crust where plates collide causes it to crack (faulting) and buckle into folds.

Fold mountains

Ocean trench
The oceanic plate is being forced under the continental plate, forming a trench. The deepest ocean trench is the Marianas Trench in the Pacific Ocean. It is 11 033 m deep

Ocean trench

Oceanic crust

Continental crust

Convection currents in the mantle cause plates to move away.

The Himalayas were formed when the Indian Plate collided with the Eurasian Plate. This process is continuing, and the Himalayas are still growing!

Earthquake centres

Melting of plate

Subduction
The oceanic plate descends because it has a higher density than the continental plate. The zone where it descends is called the **subduction zone.**

Melting crust

CONVERGENCE ZONE

8 Background reading

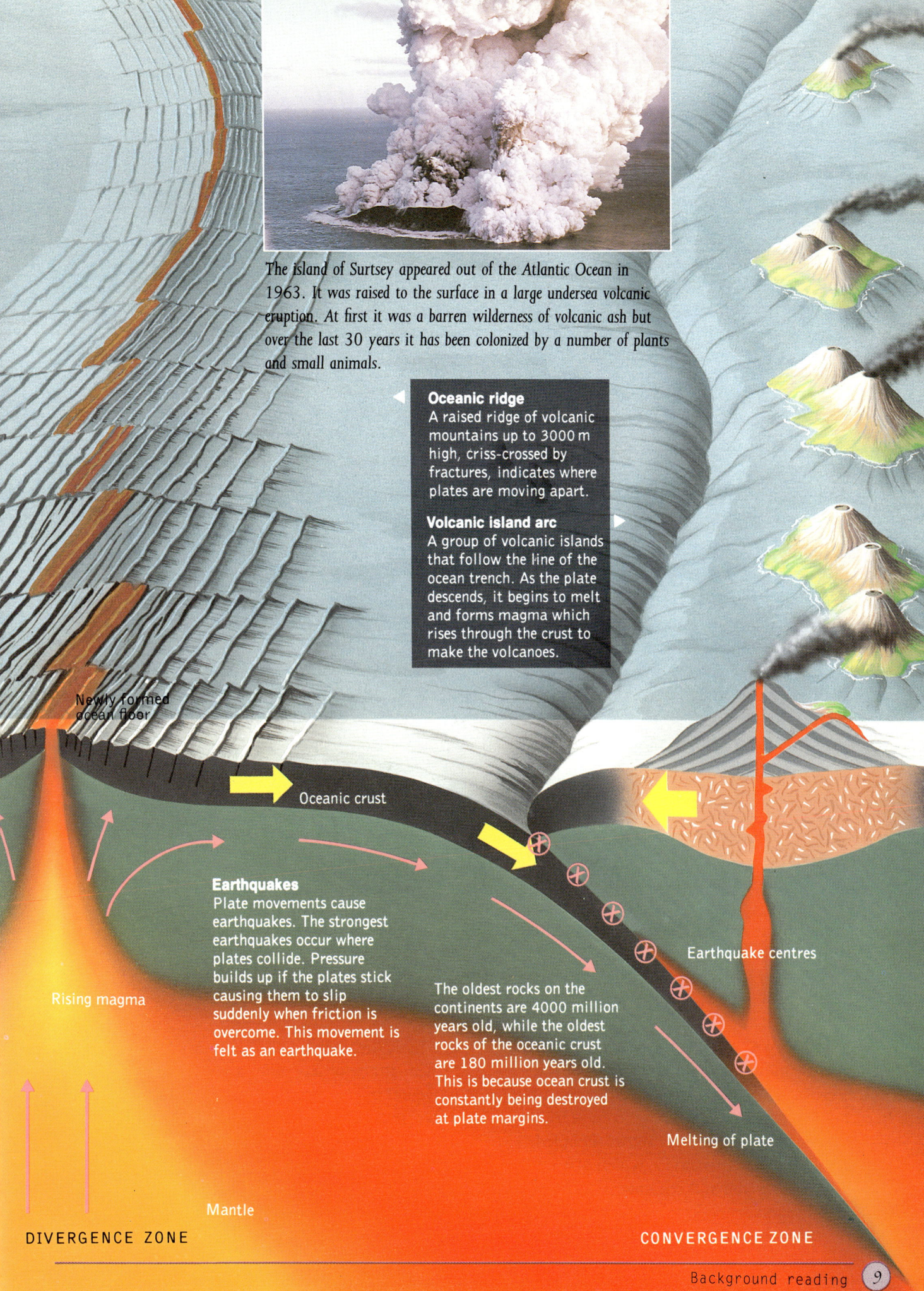

The dynamic Earth

Questions and activities

A This aerial photograph shows a fault line where two plates have slipped sideways after an earthquake. Use the maps on pages 6 and 7 to answer these questions. You will also need a school atlas for the names of towns and countries.

• Make a copy of this chart and fill it in.

High risk of earthquakes	Low risk of earthquakes
1 West coast of USA (California)	1 Great Britain
2	2
3	3
4	4
5	5

• The Himalayas were formed when the Indian plate collided with the Eurasian plate. Find two other mountain ranges which have been formed by two plates colliding together. Illustrate your answer with diagrams showing the plate movements.
• Find examples of islands which have been formed by new rock coming up as plates move apart. Describe what happens with diagrams.

Mark the locations of all your answers on a world map.

B This map and the sectional diagram show some of the features along the coast of a continent. Make a copy of the section into your notebooks. Use your diagram to answer the questions by adding to it.
• Study the features labelled A–C on the map, and decide what they are. Pick your answers from this list.

**fold mountain range   oceanic plate   volcano
fault line   deep sea trench   mid-oceanic ridge**

• Use arrows to show the direction of movement of the plates.
• Mark two places where you would find newly formed rock.
• Underneath the diagram write out this sentence and complete it:
  Two dangers faced by the town are . . .

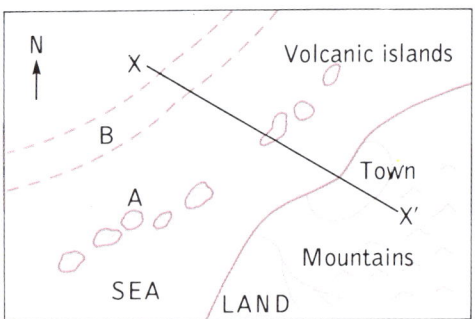

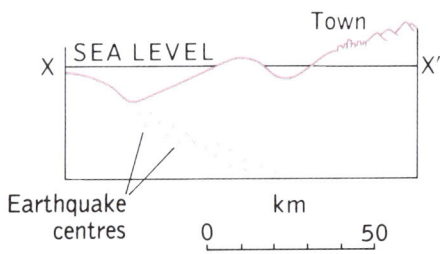

Section along the line X–X' on the map above.

C The theory of plate tectonics is now accepted as explaining many of the features of the Earth's crust. However, many other theories have been put forward in the past. One common idea was that the Earth was contracting as it cooled, causing wrinkles on the surface which cast up sea beds to form dry land and crumpled rocks into mountain ranges.

• Why is the contraction theory not adequate to explain all the observations about the crust and its movements?
• Research and write an article on the ideas about the Earth's crust and interior that came before plate tectonics, and the revolution in thinking that the plate tectonic theory caused.

Are we drifting apart?

The similarity of the coastlines of South America and Africa had been noted as far back as the 17th century, but it took developments in science and technology to develop a sound theory and build up evidence of crust movements. The evidence for continental drift was put forward by Alfred Wegener in 1912, although it was not generally accepted until the 1960s, after his death.

According to plate tectonics, the Atlantic Ocean is widening. South America and Africa are slowly drifting apart, but the movement is too slow to detect. Proving the theory means looking for *indirect* evidence.

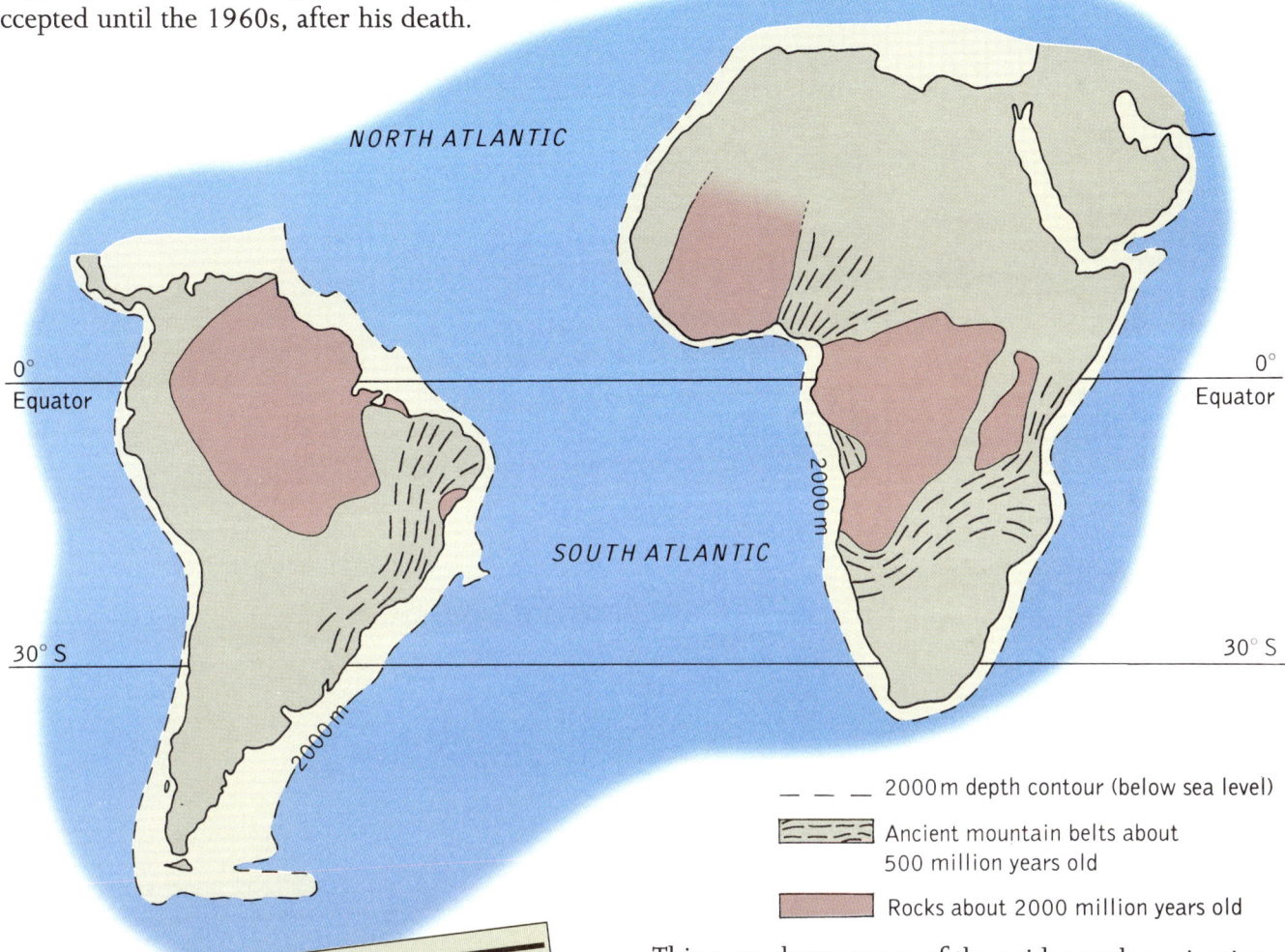

- - - 2000m depth contour (below sea level)

Ancient mountain belts about 500 million years old

Rocks about 2000 million years old

This map shows some of the evidence that scientists have used to build up the theory of continental drift. For example the shape of the two continents is a strong clue. South America fits into Africa, suggesting that they were once joined together. You will be able to find several other clues on the map.

America moving away from Britain!
From *The Comet*'s science correspondent Tex Tonics.

Scientists have come up with the startling new theory that the continents are moving apart. The movement is very slow - the Atlantic Ocean has widened by only 40km in the last 2 million years! This theory could explain many features of our planet, such as the cause of earthquakes and volcanoes, and the growth of mountains . . .

● Write an article that could have appeared in a newspaper in the 1920s, soon after the theory was first put forward. Use the map on this page as one of your illustrations.

Begin your article by giving a brief outline of the theory. You will have to do some research to collect the facts. Follow it up by pointing out the evidence for the theory that is shown on the map.

Rocks and fossils

Cliff peril

The Earth's surface is constantly changing, although usually very slowly. However around the coast of Britain you can see changes within a human lifetime.

A Suggest reasons to explain why this building is disappearing into the sea. What steps could be taken to protect the coastline?

B Make a list of other changes in the Earth's surface that could occur during your lifetime.

C Describe some changes that take place over longer periods of time.

Visual stimulus

Rocks and fossils

Rocks

If you dig a hole in your garden you will reach solid rock. This may be very close to the surface or it may be a long way down. There are many different rocks found in Britain. Here are some of the more common ones.

IGNEOUS   Granite   Basalt

SEDIMENTARY   Sandstone   Limestone

METAMORPHIC   Slate   Marble

A Study each of these rocks and look for any of them being used in local buildings. Banks and churches are good places to start.

B Find out what types of rocks occur in your area. Choose one building which has rocks not found locally. Find out where they came from and how they were used.

C Make a table of the main features of the rocks on this page. Use your observations to make a key.

Visual stimulus

Rocks and fossils

Key facts: rocks and fossils

- There are three groups of rocks: **igneous**, **sedimentary** and **metamorphic**.
- Slow processes change one rock type to another.
- Fossils are the remains of organisms preserved in rock layers.
- Rocks can be dated from the types of fossils present or by the amount of radioactivity of certain elements.
- The **geological timescale** shows the order in which rocks formed through geological time.

Igneous rocks	Sedimentary rocks	Metamorphic rocks
Formed by cooling from a magma.	Formed by deposition of rock fragments and fossils.	Formed by increased temperatures and pressures changing a rock.
Made of crystals, no fossils. No layers or beds, random pattern.	Has beds or layers of grains, fragments or fossils cemented together.	Made of crystals, no fossils, layers or beds.
Examples: Basalt, granite	*Examples:* Limestone, shale, sandstone	*Examples:* Marble, quartzite, slate

The rock cycle

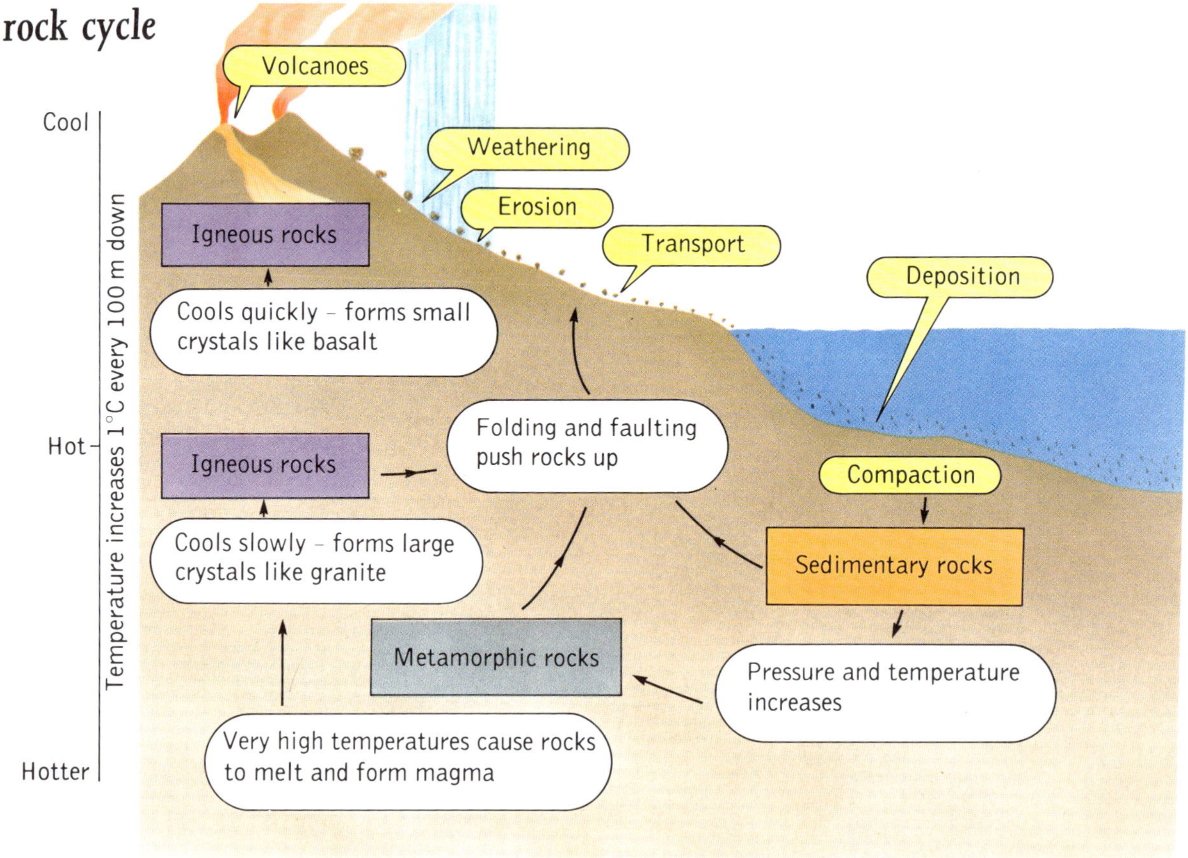

Wordwise

Volcanoes Places where magma (molten rock) erupts through the Earth's surface.

Weathering The breaking down of rocks
- *chemically*, e.g. by acidic waters affecting limestone.
- *physically*, by water in cracks freezing and expanding breaking up the rocks.

Erosion The wearing down of rocks by wind, water and ice.

Transport Eroded and weathered material are carried by wind, water and ice. The fragments are reduced in size and rounded as they are carried.

Deposition The laying down of loose sediment in rivers, deserts and the sea.

Compaction Pressure of the materials turns loose sediment into rock.

Cementation Chemicals help to stick the particles together.

Particles	→	Sedimentary rocks	→	Metamorphic rocks
Clay		Shale		Slate
Sand		Sandstone		Quartzite
Shells		Limestone		Marble

Rocks and fossils

The fossilized footprint of a dinosaur.

Dating rocks

The simplest method is to say that the rocks on top are younger than the rocks below. But this is not always true as rocks can be turned upside down by folding. Identifying fossils in the rocks can be used to work out their age. If a rock contains ammonites it must be younger than a rock that contains trilobites. These methods can only give an approximate date.

Some rocks, usually igneous rocks, contain radioactive isotopes of elements. These are unstable and decay at a constant rate. Potassium^{40} (K^{40}) decays to form Argon^{40} (Ar^{40}). The rock can be dated accurately by finding out how much of the potassium isotope has changed to argon. The more Ar^{40} there is, the older the rock.

Fossils

Fossils are the remains or traces of animals and plants. After an animal dies, its soft parts rapidly decay and the hard parts may be buried in mud or sand. Usually over many years the original shell or bone is replaced by much harder minerals, forming a fossil.
Very rarely, when there is no oxygen, some soft parts may be preserved, e.g. the Burgess shale. Sometimes only the footprints are found. Often the skeleton or shell will be broken up or dissolved so that only the imprint is left, rather like a plaster cast.

The geological timescale

The geological timescale spans about 4500 million years and is divided up into eras.

Cenozoic ('recent life') Began 66 million years ago. Mammals emerge as a diminant group. Himalayas and Alps formed

Mesozoic ('middle life') 245–55 million years ago. Began with continents joined as Pangaea and dinosaurs dominating the Earth. By the end of the Mesozoic, continents were taking their present positions and dinosaurs were extinct

Palaeozoic ('first life') 570–245 million years ago. Animals first developed hard shells, so earliest fossils date back to this era. First plants on land

Precambrian Time from formation of the Earth (about 4500 million years ago) to 570 million years ago. Very few fossils. First life on Earth about 2900 million years ago

Factfile 15

Rocks and fossils

History in the rocks

Every piece of rock tells its own story, if we know how to read the signs. By asking such questions as what the rock is made of, how old it is, whether there are any fossils and whether any crystals are visible, we can tell what type of rock it is and how it was formed.

Chalk: a sedimentary rock

Chalk is a type of soft limestone. Chemically, it is calcium carbonate (CaCO$_3$). It is made up of microscopic particles called *coccoliths*, the shelly remains of millions of tiny marine plankton. Such animals are found in the oceans today. Chalk often contains fossils of sea creatures such as bivalve molluscs and ammonites and the teeth of sharks. It

Ammonite fossils in limestone.

also contains nodules of flint. Flint is made of silica and probably comes from the remains of sponges which were dissolved and then precipitated within the chalk. Sedimentary rocks such as chalk were clearly laid down on the sea bed and must have built up as layers undisturbed over time, explaining the many fossils they contain. The layer of chalk which is found under most of England indicates that the land was once covered by a sea.

A granite 'tor' on Dartmoor.

Granite and basalt: igneous rocks

Hot magma has a low density and can force its way up (**intrude**) through the denser rocks above it. In volcanic eruptions, it escapes at the surface. Igneous rocks are formed when the magma cools. They are made of mineral crystals. The size of these crystals tells us how slowly the magma cooled. The large crystals in granite indicate very slow cooling. This happens when the magma cools deep underground because the rocks above prevent heat from escaping. The granite rocks of Dartmoor are still quite hot after millions of years: drilling down 1 km has revealed temperatures of 80°C – a possible alternative source of energy!

Basalt is composed of tiny crystals and is formed by magma which has erupted out of volcanoes and cooled quickly through exposure to the air.

Basalt columns, Giant's Causeway, Northern Ireland. Here, fast cooling not only produced the tiny basalt crystals but also caused the rock to crack into large hexagonal columns.

Marble: a metamorphic rock

Marble is a rock which can be highly polished. It is a rock which has been changed or **metamorphosed** by being subjected to high temperature and pressure. Marble started off as limestone which was deposited on a sea bed. At some point the limestone

Rocks and fossils

came into contact with high temperature, perhaps from intruding magma. This caused the structure of the rock to change. Chemically, marble is still calcium carbonate, but it has an interlocking mosaic of crystals which makes it harder and changes its appearance completely. The shelly fragments and fossils in limestone are destroyed in the process, leaving a smoother, uniform granular structure.

The Taj Mahal, faced with polished marble, was built over 300 years ago by the emperor Shah Jahan as a tomb for his wife.

Britain through time

Britain's variety of rocks and fossils show that the climate and environment have changed with time. The Earth's climate belts have not changed since they depend on the solar energy reaching the surface (see Section 4). This means Britain must have drifted across the latitudes due to plate movements.

Now	Britain has drifted North to 52°N in the temperate belt. Where next?
170 Mya*	Britain was back in the tropics at 30°N. The seas were warm and ammonite-rich shales and limestones were deposited
200 Mya	Britain was 15°N, the latitude of the Sahara Desert today. Red sandstone deposits indicate a desert landscape with huge sand dunes. Dinosaurs roamed the land, leaving their footprints and some bones
240 Mya	Britain was on the equator and covered with dense rainforests. The compressed remains of trees formed the coal deposits mined today
450 Mya	Britain was 30°S, where Australia is today. Warm shallow seas covered the country, and coral reefs existed in Shropshire!
700 Mya	Britain was near the South Pole and covered with an ice sheet that has left glacial deposits

Britain was attached to other land for most of this time

*Mya = million years ago.

A Find out about the following metamorphic rocks: slate, gneiss, quartzite, schist. For each type, say
  a what the original rock was;
  b what factors caused the change; and
  c how the new rocks differ from the old.

B Coal only forms near the Equator. Why is this? Why does Britain have coal deposits?

C List the evidence suggesting that Britain has moved from the South to the North.

Rocks and fossils

Questions and activities

A Arrange these events, oldest first, in the correct order:

First plants on land; first soft-bodied animals; first fish; first hard-bodied animals; first human beings; first life on Earth; first mammals.

B The diagram shows the steps as a shark is fossilized.

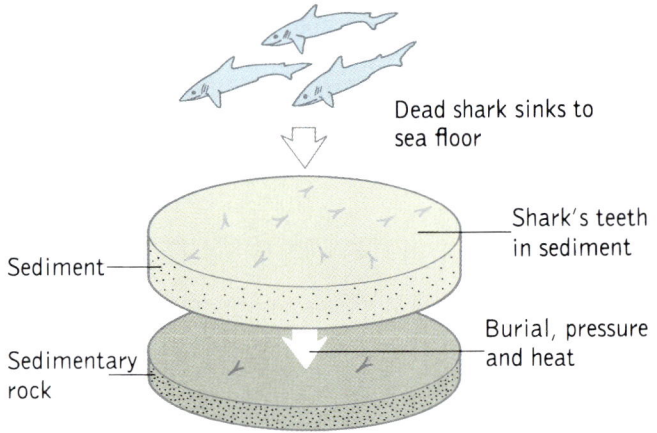

a What happens to the rest of the shark's body?
b Why are the teeth preserved?
c Few of the teeth become fossils. What could have destroyed the teeth?

C **It was a long time ago...**

David: 'It was a long time ago, about 10 years ago, that I was just a kid.'
History teacher: 'It was a long time ago that Julius Cæsar landed in Britain – about 2000 years ago.
Archaeologist: 'Stone age people were around a long time ago; about 60 000 years ago.
Science teacher: 'The granite of Dartmoor is about 250 million years old; quite new compared to the rocks in northwest Scotland, which are 2000 million years old.'

Try to display these 'long times' to scale on a chart. You could set up a time line, or make up a clock face where the whole circle depicts 2000 million years.

D Copy the table below and tick one or more boxes to complete it.

	Igneous	Sedimentary	Metamorphic
Rock contains fossils			
Rock is made of crystals			
Rock is found in beds or layers			

E A river has deposited a number of pebbles on the river bed. When the pebbles are moved they are rolled along the bottom and strike against each other. Arrange the four types of pebbles in the chart below in the correct order.

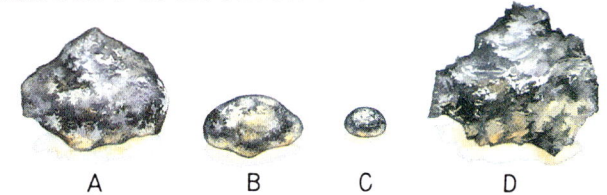

Shape	Description	Distance carrried (km)
		0.2
		0.5
		1.0
		5.0

F A block of porous rock was put into a beaker of water for 10 min. It was then put in a freezer for 24 hours and then defrosted. This process was repeated three times. The rock cracked and completely disintegrated. Explain why the rock fell apart.

G Make a collection of rocks. Try to include some from different parts of the country. Can you find examples from each of the three main groups?

For each of the rocks find out if it is ever used for building in your area. What properties of the rock affect whether it can be used for building or not?

H Geological processes are very slow. It can take centuries for a change to become apparent. Work out the following:
● At the present time sediment is being deposited in the Pacific Ocean at a rate of 2 cm every 1000 years.
a How long will it take to form a bed of sediment 30 cm thick?
b How thick a layer will be formed over a period of a million years?

● Look at gravestones near to your school. The words on the older stones will be very difficult to read. Calculate how fast they are wearing away.
● Snowdon is 1085 m high. If the erosion rate is 2 mm/year how long will it take to erode down to sea level?

Plan and make a video

You have been asked to make a video to teach students about the rock cycle. You will probably be able to do this better in large groups, with the work shared out. You will need to
● make sure each person knows their responsibilities;
● research the material you wish to include;
● make collections of appropriate rocks;
● make suitable posters, exhibits and models;
● decide on any dialogue, interviews, presenters and commentators;
● write a script if necessary;
● make a storyboard of the sequences required in the video;
● film the different sequences to make the video.

Water and stone

Water, water everywhere...

Household water in Britain comes from a variety of sources. Some places use natural rivers or lakes. Others save water in artificial reservoirs, or use water piped up from underground wells.

Water Rationing!

'Water levels in our reservoirs are the lowest we have ever known. Unless there is substantial rainfall soon rationing will have to be imposed.'

said a spokesman from the Water Authority. Last winter was very dry so the reservoirs were not full when summer began. The hose pipe ban may last throughout next winter.

Safety warning

Nitrate levels in the reservoirs have built up as water has evaporated. In turn this has caused the growth of poisonous algae. Several dogs have become ill after swimming in reservoirs. As a precaution all water sports have now been banned.

All around the region, rivers are beginning to run dry. This is not only because of the poor rainfall. As the population has grown, more water has been taken from the ground for people to use.

A Find out how your locality gets its water. How is it collected? How is it treated to make it drinkable? Has your area had water restrictions? Are there any plans to improve the situation?

B How much water could you save? Use these sample figures to estimate the amount you use normally, and then look at ways you could save water without risking your health!

Bath 80 l; shower 30 l; flushing toilet 10 l; washing up in a bowl 10 l; dishwasher 50 l; washing car with hose 100 l; 1 day's cooking and drinking 6 l; 1 washing machine load 100 l.

Water and stone

Quarries – assets or liabilities?

In Britain there are quarries for coal, brick clay, building stone, road stone, sand and gravels, slate, cement and iron ore. We must have these materials, but few people enjoy living near a quarry.

An opencast coal pit.

Limestone quarry blasted into a hillside.

A sand quarry.

A What are the nearest quarries to your area? With your class, discuss the importance of the quarries to the local economy.

B What problems would people who lived near the quarries shown in these photographs face? Make suggestions that could reduce some of the problems.

C When quarries are finished with, something useful has to be done with the land. Find out what uses people find for worked out quarries.

Visual stimulus 21

Water and stone

Key facts: water and stone

- The Sun's heat causes water to **evaporate** from lakes and seas, and from the ground. This water later **condenses** into clouds. Rain falls back to the surface (**precipitation**). The same water goes round and round. This is called the **water cycle**.
- Only the water evaporates from the sea. Salt and other impurities are left behind, so rainwater is always fresh. This is the source of our drinking water.
- Many forms of rock are used for making building materials. Frost and rain can wear away these building materials in time, especially those made from soft sedimentary rocks.
- Limestone is made of calcium carbonate. It is easily dissolved by acids in rain. Natural carbon dioxide from the air forms a weak acid when dissolved, and sulphur dioxide pollution in the air makes rain even more acidic.

The water cycle

The energy which powers the water cycle comes from the Sun. The heat of the Sun **evaporates** water from the ground, from lakes and rivers, and from the seas. Water vapour rises up through the atmosphere until it reaches a cold layer of air. It then **condenses** into droplets of water. Eventually these fall to the ground as rain or snow. This is called **precipitation**.

The water from rain or snow trickles downhill, collecting into streams and rivers. Finally it runs into the sea, where it will stay until the Sun evaporates it again. The cycle is complete.

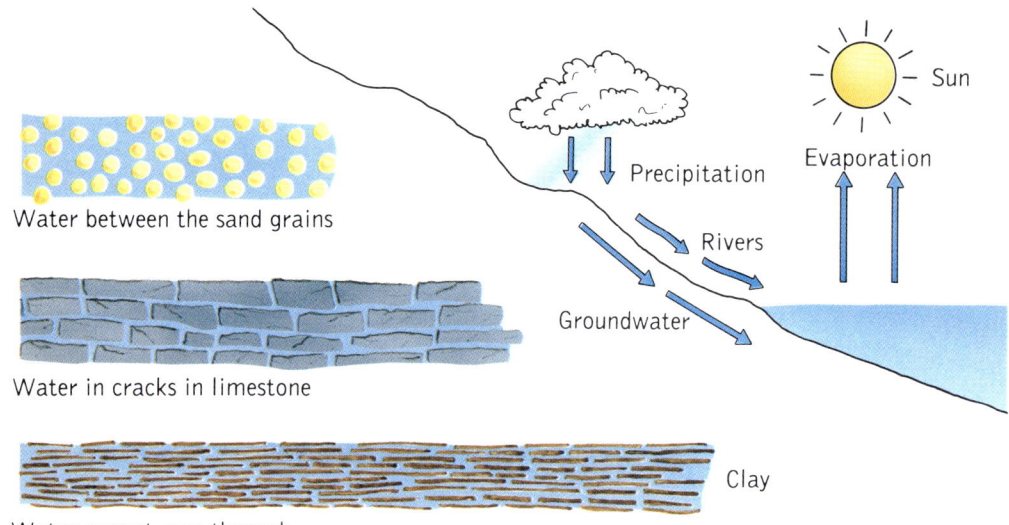

When water evaporates from the sea the salt is left behind. The clouds and rain always contain fresh water.

Salty or fresh?

Most of the world's water is found in the oceans, and is too salty to drink. Only 2.4% is fresh.

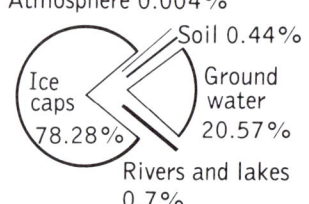

How the world's fresh water is divided up.

Drinking water

Most drinking water comes from wells which bring up water from under the ground. Rainwater trickles down into porous rocks such as sandstone and chalk. If there is a layer of **impermeable** rock (rock that water cannot penetrate) underneath, such as clay, the water will be trapped. The water is held in the porous rock and forms an **aquifer** – a water-bearing rock. Wells drilled into aquifers may be up to 200 m deep.

Surface water may be stored in lakes and reservoirs. River water is also used. The river Thames runs through Oxford, Reading and London. Water is taken out at the first town and is filtered and cleaned chemically to make it drinkable. After it has been used it goes into the sewers. At the sewage farm it is filtered and cleaned again. Then it goes back into the river, ready for use in the next town. By the time the water finally runs into the sea it may have been drunk by seven people!

Water and stone

Rocks for building

Fragments of basalt are often mixed with tar to give a tough road surface with plenty of grip. This mixture is called TarMacadam – tarmac for short. Igneous rocks such as granite can also be used for building, although it is very expensive because it is so hard to cut. The city of Edinburgh is famous for its granite buildings.

Sedimentary rocks such as limestone and sandstone are softer and easier to cut into shape. Many important buildings such as the Houses of Parliament and St Paul's Cathedral are faced with Portland Limestone, which is quarried in Dorset. It is soft enough to carve into beautiful shapes, but hard enough not to crumble. Sadly one big disadvantage has shown up in modern times. All limestones are made of calcium carbonate, so the acid rain formed by polluted city air easily dissolves most types away, although Portland stone is quite resistant.

Slate is a metamorphic rock which splits naturally into thin sheets, so it is suitable for roof coverings.

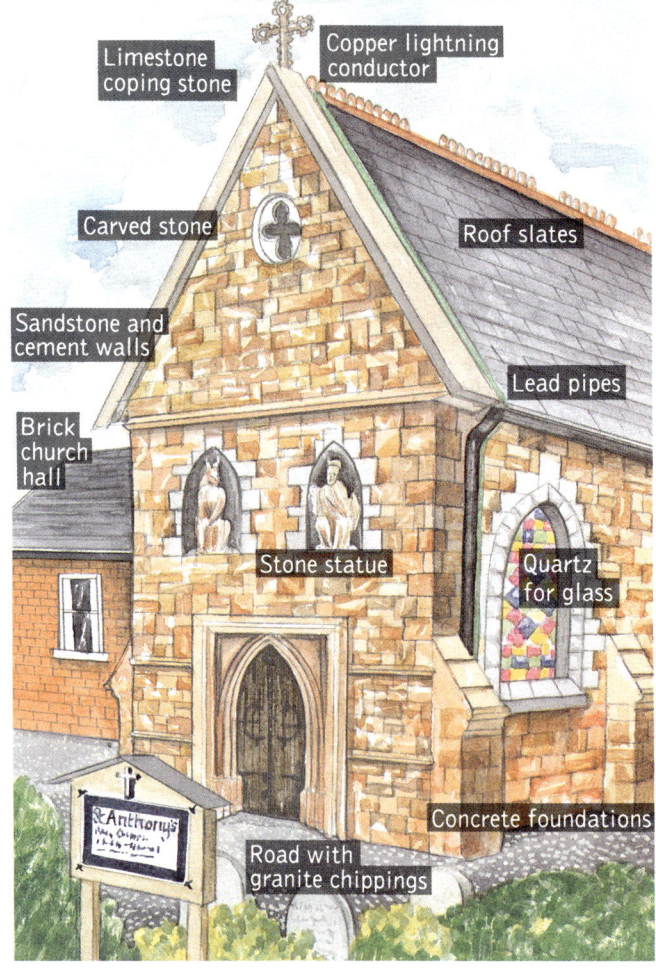

One building needs rock from many sources.

Using minerals

Gypsum, $CaSO_4 \cdot 2H_2O$: To thicken paint, toothpaste and paper. Plaster and Plaster of Paris are made from it.

Halite (salt), NaCl: To preserve and flavour food. To melt ice on roads. As raw material for hydrochloric acid (HCl) and sodium hydroxide (NaOH).

Fluorite, CaF_2: For 'fluoride' in toothpaste and drinking water. Raw material for hydrofluoric acid (HF).

Quartz, SiO_2: Glass manufacture. Silicon chips. Sandpaper.

Factfile

Water and stone

Leaking rocks

Some rocks have no spaces to contain water and they do not allow water to pass through them. These are **impermeable** rocks. Igneous and metamorphic rocks are usually impermeable and so is shale, the fine-grained clay-rich sedimentary rock. Most sandstones can hold water and so are porous. Water is able to pass between the grains in these permeable rocks. This property is important when considering water supplies, waste disposal and major engineering projects.

The leaking dam

The Glen Canyon Dam in the desert state of Arizona is a concrete dam, 218 m high, that dams the Colorado river. The rock on which it is built is Navajo sandstone. This is strong enough to support the dam, but being porous allows water to seep through the sandstone. To avoid the rock becoming unstable the sandstone around the dam is bolted together with steel bolts 20 m long.

The leaking tunnel

The main railway line from Bristol to South Wales crosses under the river Severn in a tunnel about 8 km long. It was completed in 1886 but its construction had been very difficult due to problems of flooding. The tunnel runs through a soft impermeable clay and crosses a fault line. Here water leaks from a porous sandstone which is full of water. By 1929 the tunnel was flooding with river water. Eight thousand tons of cement was pumped into the surrounding rocks to stop the leaking. Railway workers patrolled the river looking

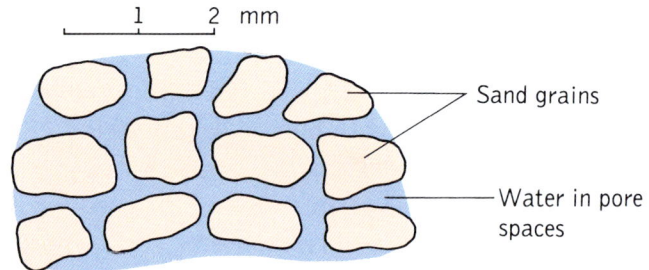

Close-up view of porous sandstone.

Glen Canyon Dam in Arizona.

leaking. Railway workers patrolled the river looking for places where cement came to the surface. Where it did they placed a layer of clay on the river bed to stop river water entering the tunnel. The repairs worked until the 1980s when the leakage began again. Again cement has been injected into the rocks to seal the gaps, strengthen the rocks and keep the water out.

> **A** Try to explain each of the following: why the Glen Canyon Dam was built on permeable rock; why some canals and ponds are lined with clay; why tunnels in igneous rocks rarely leak.
>
> **B** Read the passage about the Severn tunnel. Why did the workers pump cement into the surrounding rocks? What properties of cement make this a suitable material?
>
> **C** A chemical company is looking for a disused quarry where they can dispose of waste chemicals. What type of quarry would be the most suitable?

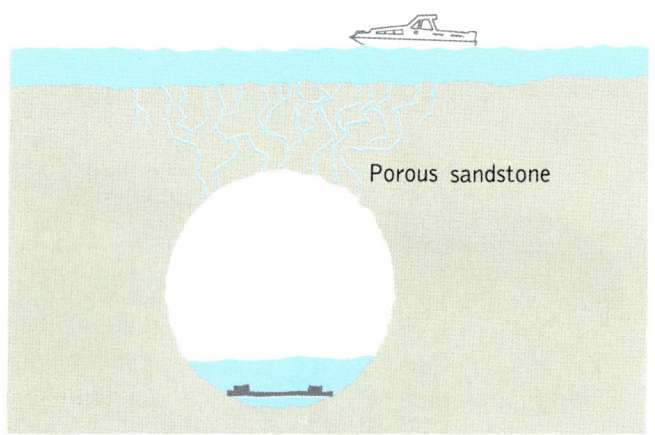

Problems with tunnels passing through sandstone.

These boats have been left stranded many miles from the Aral Sea.

A new dead sea

The Aral Sea is an inland sea in the Soviet Union. It is fed by two long rivers, the Amu Darya 2500 km long and the Syr Darya 2200 km long. The lake is in a very dry area and the two rivers are the main source of water to the lake. Water can only leave by evaporation.

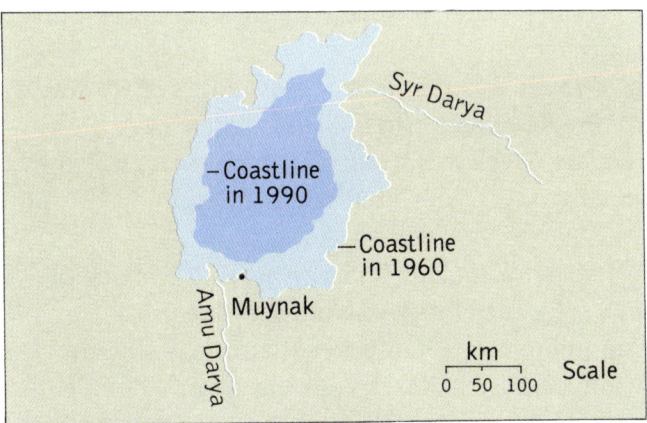

In 1918 major irrigation projects were started hundreds of kilometres from the Aral Sea. They used the water from the two rivers to grow 90% of the country's cotton as well as cereal and melons. Now the Amu Darya is dry before it reaches the Aral Sea and the Syr Darya is reduced to a trickle.

The Aral Sea is shrinking leaving behind salt wastelands. It could disappear within 30 years.

Twenty-five years ago Muynak was a fishing port with 10 000 fishermen working in the Aral Sea. Now it is 32 km from the edge of the sea and the fishing boats are abandoned in the sand. The pike, perch and bream along with 24 other species of fish have disappeared as the salt concentration increases. Even the climate has changed with colder winters and hotter summers. When the wind blows 43 million tons of gritty salt a year are picked up and carried over the towns and fields.

The water in the wells is now salty and often undrinkable so the freshwater supply has become critical. The fields grow poor crops with low yields as the level of the salt has increased. The people who live there suffer from a high rate of respiratory diseases and throat cancer.

- Produce a chart to show what the water cycle used to be like for the region. Show on the chart what has happened to cause the changes. Discuss what steps could be taken to save the Aral Sea.

Background reading 25

Water and stone

Questions and activities

A Match the words in the list below to the definitions:

**well   dam   spring   precipitation
water table   aquifer**

- level of water in the rocks below ground;
- underground water which comes to the surface naturally;
- rocks which provide a supply of underground water;
- a deep hole through which underground water can be obtained;
- wall of earth or concrete that holds water back;
- all water falling from the atmosphere as rain, sleet or snow.

B The geological section below shows a source of supply of underground water.

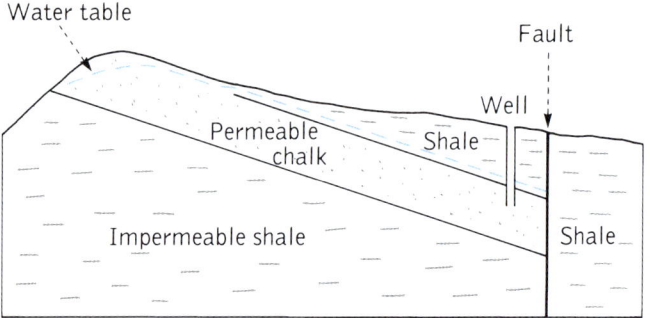

a Draw a similar diagram and label the rock containing water and the source of a spring.
b At the position of the well in your drawing would there be a good water supply?
c Suggest two reasons for the water table being lowered.

C Draw a pie chart to show the average household water used per person per day, using the data below:

WC flushing	32%
Washing machine	12%
Bath/shower	17%
Washing cars/garden	3%
Washing up/cooking	36%

We use about 130 l per day. What happens to all this water when it goes down the drain?

D Study the diagram below.

Water companies
1 Northumbria
2 North West
3 York
4 Severn-Trent
5 Anglian
6 Wales
7 Thames
8 Southern
9 Wessex
10 South West

Water supply
Ground water   Surface water

Underground and surface water supplies in England and Wales.

a Which water company uses most underground water?
b Which water company uses most surface water?
c Predict which parts of the country have high rainfall. Check this from information on rainfall in an atlas. Were your predictions correct?

E The Parthenon is falling apart. It is made of blocks of limestone but they are just crumbling away. Rainwater is normally slightly acidic because it mixes with the carbon dioxide in air to form a weak acid. The usual pH is 5-6 but in parts of Europe it can be as low as 3. The acid rain reacts with limestone causing it to dissolve.

a Find out what is causing the very acid rain that falls on the Parthenon.
b Suggest some ways in which it may be possible to preserve buildings affected by weathering.

Quarries and waste

Disused quarries appear to be ideal places for getting rid of household rubbish. Old quarries may be dangerous or eyesores. They often collect rainwater and lakes can form in them. After the quarry has been filled with waste the site could form a clear flat park or playing field.

Bedton Borough Council has put forward proposals to use a local quarry for waste disposal. The council has asked for comments on the proposals.

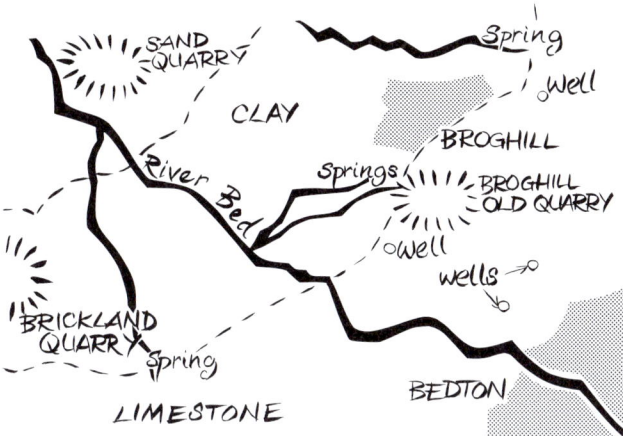

Bedton and Broghill.

a Make a list of all the types of waste that goes into your bins at home. Which materials will decay or decompose? Which ones could be recycled?

b What do you think leachate is? Find out by checking in books on geology if you are correct.

c Prepare two cases for the next council meeting
 • giving reasons for allowing the quarry to be used for waste disposal;
 • explaining why it should not be used for this purpose.

d Suggest alternative uses for the old quarry.

e Study the map of the area. Can you suggest a more suitable site for waste disposal?

Bedton Water Company

Proposal 67/2x/651: Waste disposal

We do not object to this proposal but you will need to carry out a series of surveys in order to ensure that the underlying rocks can be sealed against any danger of leachate leaking into our wells nearby. You will be required to monitor all water flows in and out around the site.

Yours faithfully,
D Kaye
Hydrogeologist

Scrapmetals
Copper Recycling Ltd

Dear sir

Proposal 67/2x/651: Waste disposal

My company would be very interested in developing this site as a potential methane gas source. We would like to use the gas to generate electricity at our workshops in Broghill. Please do contact us to discuss this possibility.
Yours faithfully,
CH Fore

Dear Sir,

We the residents of Broghill do not want a tip nearby. It would smell foul, litter would blow round the village and we would be disturbed by noisy, heavy trucks. We have also heard that methane gas can collect underground which can cause explosions.

Yours in disgust
The residents of Broghill

Dear Councillors,
It is clear from your recent proposals that you are unaware that the Broghill quarry is the only site in Bedton where the Great Crested Newt and toads are still found. The old quarry now has a wide range of plants and animals. This site should be protected not destroyed.
Yours sincerely
Eleanor Bradley

The Earth and its climate

The spinning Earth

The Earth is spinning on its own axis. At the same time, it is orbiting the Sun. It takes 1 day for the Earth to rotate once on its own axis and 1 year to make the journey round the Sun.

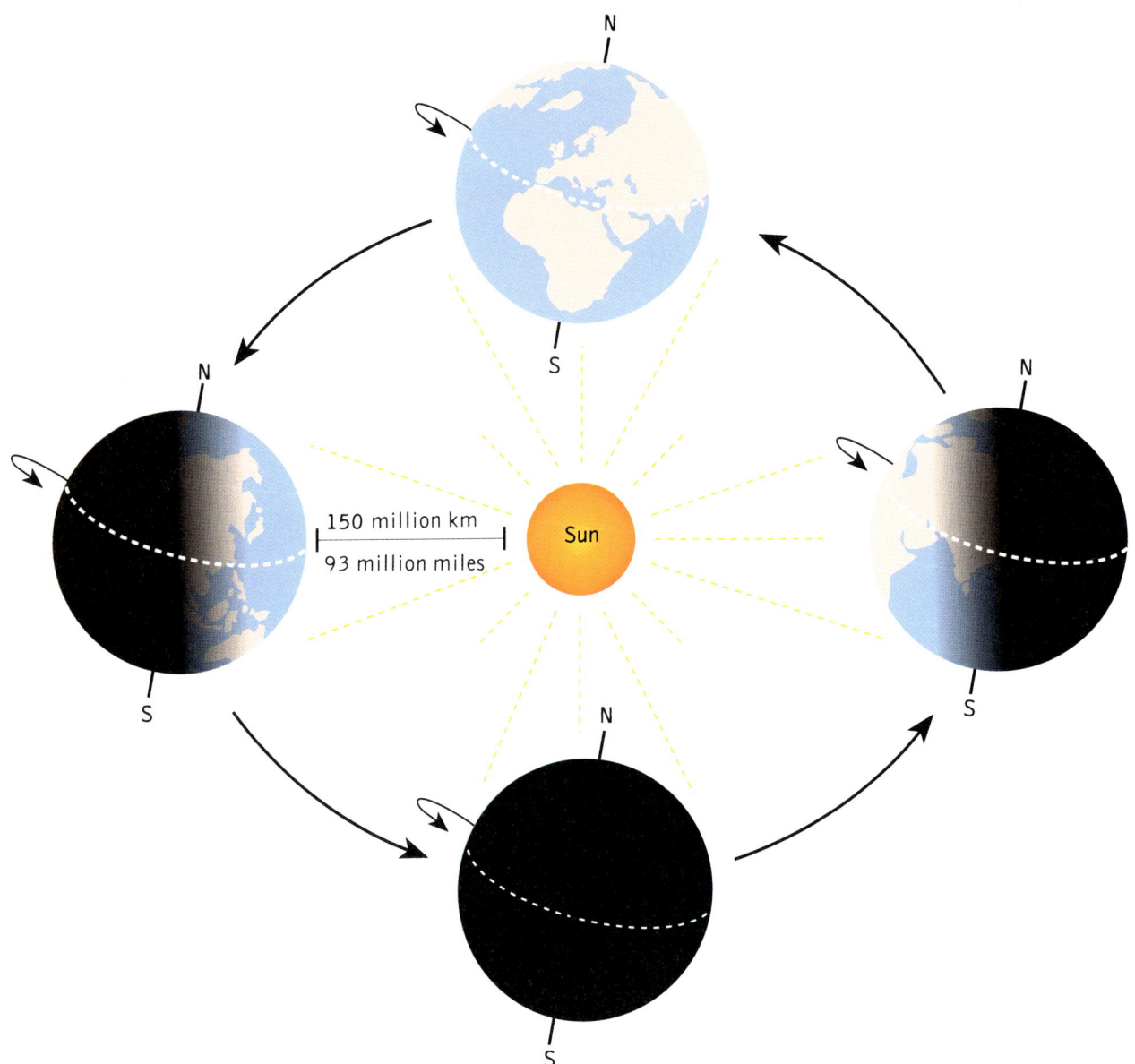

A Since it takes a year for the Earth to travel around the Sun, how far will it have moved in
a one day
b one month?

B Use the diagrams to work out
a why each 24 hour period is divided into daylight and darkness;
b why in Britain there are fewer hours of daylight in winter than in summer;

C Make a model of the Sun and the Earth. Use this to explain to others in your group:
a day and night;
b day length;
c changes in the inclination of the Sun.

Visual stimulus

The Earth and its climate

Seasonal changes

In Britain, the weather changes with the seasons. Countries close to the Equator have similar weather all year.

Spring.

Summer.

Autumn.

Winter.

A Describe the kind of weather you would expect in spring, summer, autumn and winter. Suppose you have been unconscious for many years. When you recover you have no idea of the date. What clues could tell you the time of the year? Make a list of your ideas for each season.

B Imagine you are at the North Pole. Draw four pictures of what you would expect the surroundings to look like in March, June, September and December.

How would this be different if you were at
a the South Pole; **b** the Equator.

Visual stimulus 29

The Earth and its climate

Key facts: the Earth and its climate

- The climate is affected by the amount of heat reaching the surface of the Earth.
- It is hotter near the Equator because more of the Sun's energy reaches the surface.
- It takes approximately 1 month for the Moon to travel round the Earth.
- The pull of gravity between the Earth, Sun and Moon causes tides.
- Weather fronts are caused by moving masses of air.
- Both cold and warm fronts bring bad weather.

Phases of the Moon

The Moon gives out no light of its own but reflects the light from the Sun. As the Moon travels round the Earth it also rotates on its own axis, so that the same surface is always facing us; the other side of the Moon has only been seen by astronauts. It takes 28 days (one lunar month) for the Moon to orbit the Earth. The phases of the Moon are caused by different amounts of its sunlit surface being visible from Earth.

The inner circle in the diagram shows the sunlit surface of the Moon. The outer circle shows the Moon as it would appear from Earth.

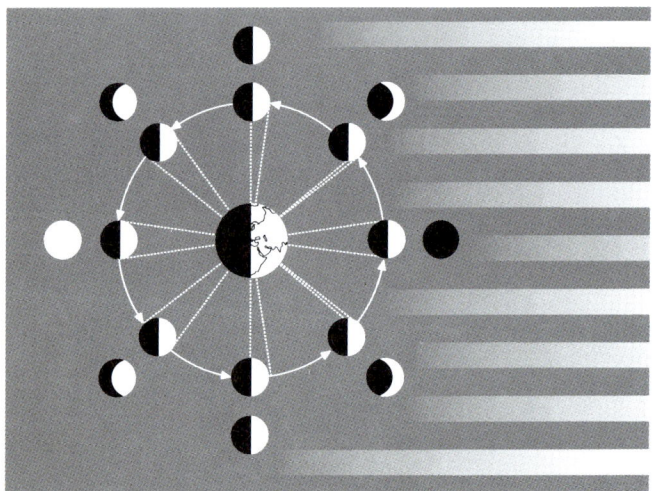

Variation in solar energy

The amount of heat energy received by the Earth is greater in the tropics than at the Poles. As you travel away from the Equator the amount of heat reaching Earth is spread over a larger area. This makes the climate of the tropics warmer than the climates of regions further north and south.

Weather symbols

Here are some of the symbols used to record or forecast the weather.

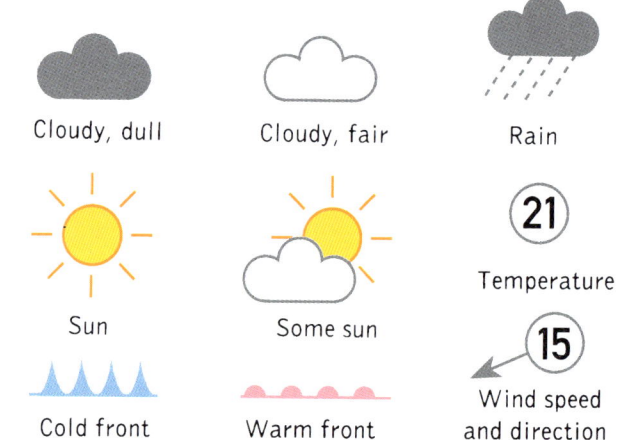

Tides

Although the Moon is much smaller than the Earth, it exerts a gravitational force which causes tides to occur. As the Moon travels round the Earth, the Oceans are pulled towards it. The same force is exerted on land but the effect is not as noticeable. In some regions the tide can be as much as 12 m while on land it is more like 15 cm. The Sun has a similar effect and when the Sun and Moon are in line, much greater tides are recorded. These are the Spring tides. The lowest or 'Neap' tides occur when the pull of the Moon and Sun are at right angles, reducing the overall effect.

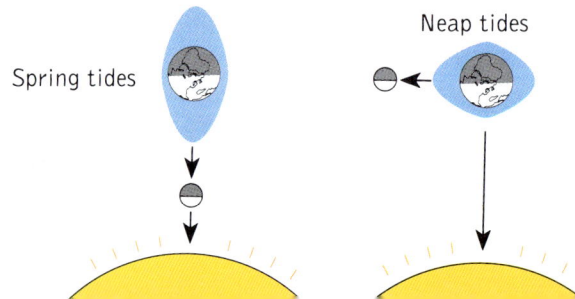

The Earth and its climate

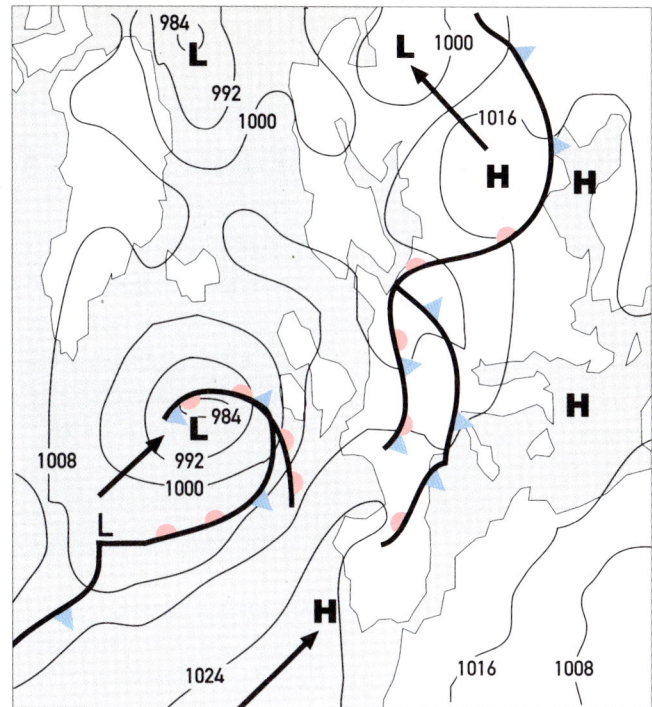

Weather maps

A weather map tells you what the weather is like over different parts of the country and what changes may take place. You need to know the direction and speed at which air masses are moving.

The normal atmospheric pressure is referred to as 1 atmosphere or 1000 **millibars** (mb). The lower the number below this the lower the pressure. If the number is greater than 1000 it will indicate high pressure. A **low** or **depression** is a region with pressure lower than its surroundings. This is also called a **cyclone**. A **high** or **anticyclone** is a region of atmospheric pressure higher than its surroundings.

A **cold front** is caused by an advancing mass of cold air while a **warm front** is caused by an advancing mass of warm air. Cold fronts bring colder air with good visibility and showers. Warm fronts bring warmer air with poor visibility and rain from continuous cloud cover. **Occlusions** are regions where warm and cold fronts mix and bring variable weather activity.

Movement of fronts

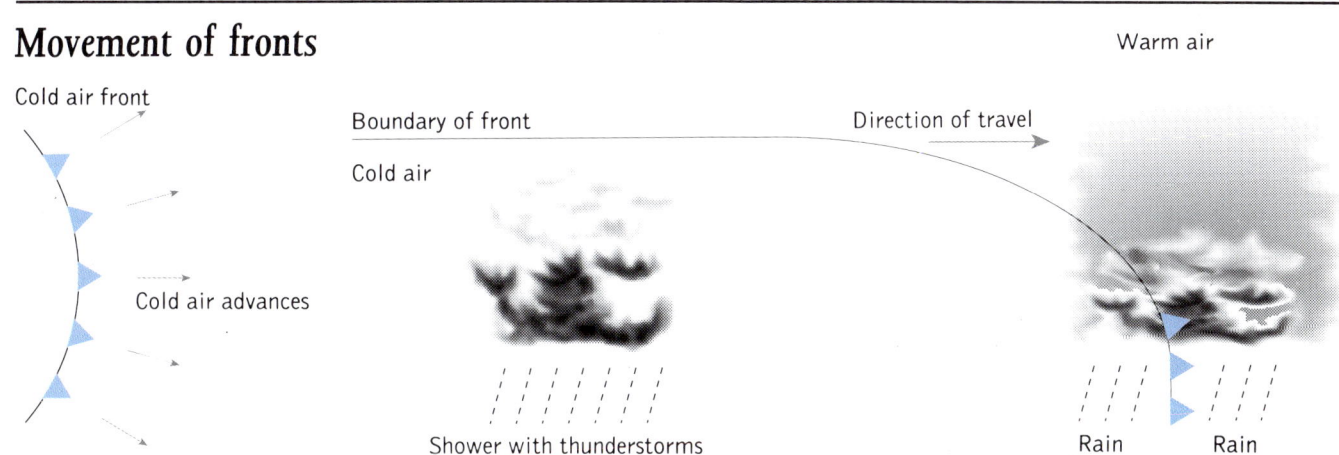

The cold air is heavier and as it advances it moves under the warm air pushing it up in the process.

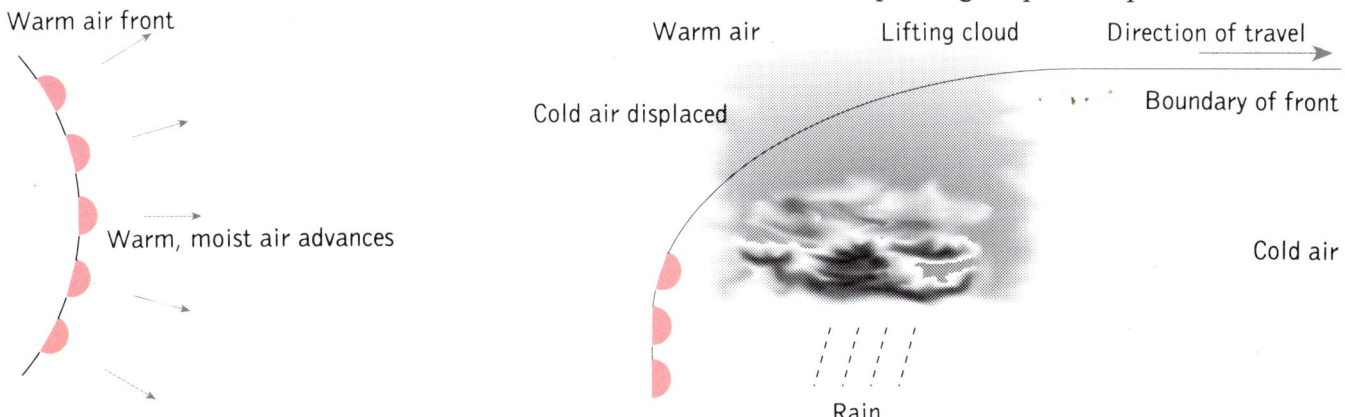

The less dense warm air moves up over the cold air. The cold air lies underneath and is only pushed back very slowly.

Factfile

The Earth and its climate

From breezes to hurricanes

When a balloon bursts, air rushes out causing a loud bang. This happens because the air inside the balloon is at a higher pressure than the air outside. As soon as it can escape, the air moves rapidly to equalize the different pressures. Winds are also caused by air moving from regions of high to low pressure.

What causes the high and low pressures?

Hot air rises. Air rising will create a region of low pressure and cold air will move in to take its place. In the eighteenth century, George Hadley thought that the hot air over the Equator would rise and flow north and south sinking down over the poles and returning to the Equator to be warmed again. However it is a long way from the Equator to the Poles and the air will have cooled down long before it gets to the North and South Poles. The actual pattern of air movement is more complicated as you can see from the diagram.

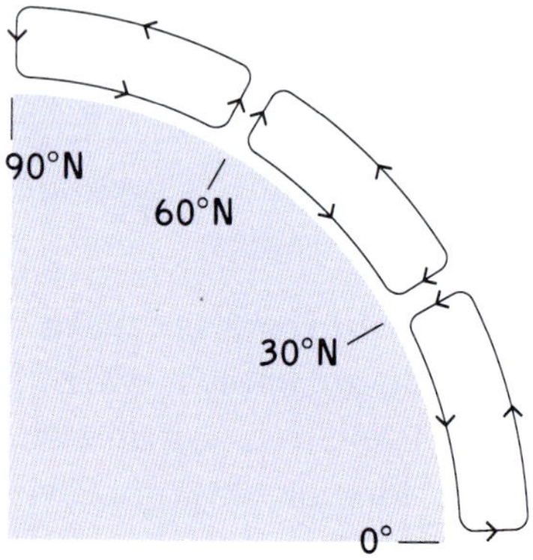

The Earth's rotation

Wind movements are complicated further because the Earth and its atmosphere are moving at over 1500 km/h at the Equator but stationary at the poles. This causes the winds to be deflected to the right in the northern hemisphere and to the left in the southern hemisphere. A wind blowing north over Europe will be deflected to the east as a result of the Earth's rotation. A wind blowing south will be deflected to the west because it cannot move as fast as the Earth is rotating. It gets left behind!

Weather map showing isobars.

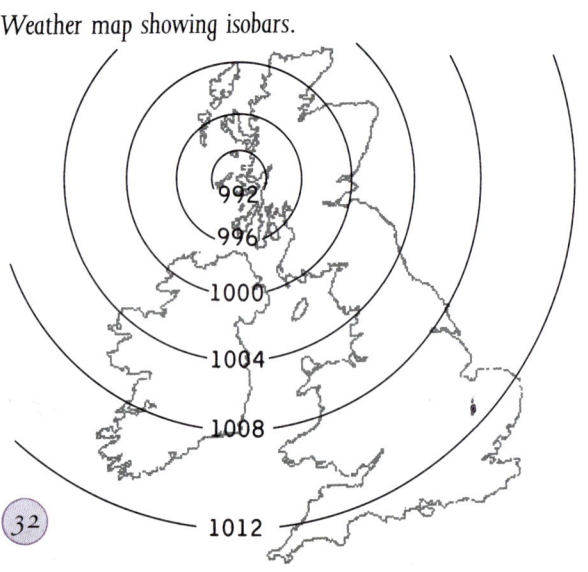

Hurricane Elena photographed by the Space Shuttle Discovery.

The pattern of air movement between the Equator and the North Pole.

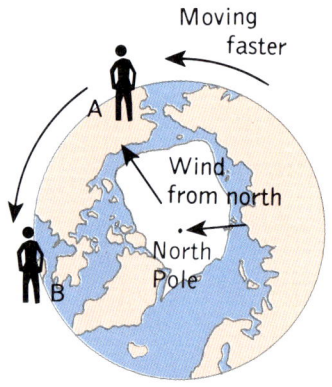

By the time the wind gets to point A, you will now be at point B so the wind has been deflected to the left.

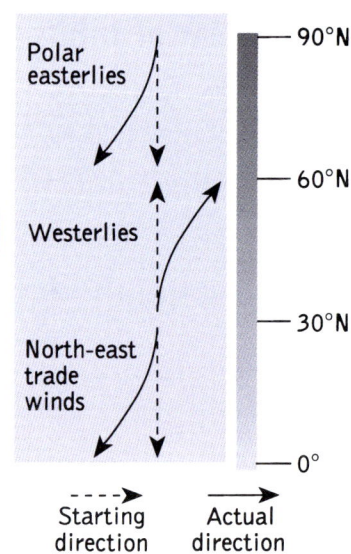

Wind speeds

If you study a weather map, you will see lines drawn across it called **isobars**. These are lines joining points of equal pressure. If these lines are close together there will be strong winds. The winds will be moving into areas of low pressure. Gales are more likely to be severe in the winter due to the bigger temperature differences between the Equator and the polar regions. This will cause lower or deeper depressions and air will rush in more quickly to equalize the pressures.

Background reading

The Earth and its climate

Wind direction

A wind takes its name from where it comes from. 'The north wind doth blow and we shall have snow' goes the rhyme, telling us that this wind is blowing down from the Arctic. In Britain our weather is affected by depressions forming over the Atlantic, where cold air from the north meets warm air from further south.

On December 1, 1966, a very deep depression occurred with a central pressure of 943 millibars (mb), one of the deepest known to have crossed this country. Severe gales, hail, thunder, snow and tornadoes accompanied it across most of the British Isles. The October 1987 storm which caused such massive destruction was also caused by a very deep depression.

Winds and climate

Air which rises gives low pressure and tends to result in wet, unsettled weather. As the air rises it cools, decreasing the amount of water it can hold. This will result in clouds forming and rain may follow. Heavy rainfall can result in flooding, damaging crops and buildings.

Sinking air gives high pressure. Such features are called anticyclones and they give dry, settled weather. The sinking air becomes warmer increasing the amount of water it can hold. Clouds and rain will be less likely. This can result in long summer droughts.

A The southernmost part of Britain is at 50° latitude. Use information provided in this section to work out the approximate speed you would be moving if you lived in Cornwall.

B Look at the diagrams which show the wind movements in the northern hemisphere. From this work out the likely wind patterns in the southern hemisphere. Use an atlas which shows a map of the major wind patterns. Does this agree with your predictions?

C Winds do not blow directly into an area of low pressure. In the northern hemisphere, the winds rotate anticlockwise round a depression.

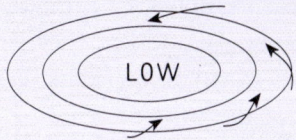

Study the information of how the Earth's rotation affects wind movement and then explain this. What would you expect to happen to the winds in a region of high pressure?

D Thunderstorms occur when a volume of warm air rises quickly drawing in a large amount of moist air. Explain what will cause the heavy rainfall. Use the library to find out what causes the thunder and lightning.

The Earth and its climate

Questions and activities

A Copy this passage choosing the correct word from each pair in brackets.

The amount of heat energy reaching the Earth is (smaller/greater) in the tropics than at the poles. This means the tropics are (warmer/colder) than the poles. (Hot/cold) air (rising/sinking) over the tropics causes (colder/warmer) air to move in to take its place. Areas where hot air is rising are likely to have (unsettled/settled), (wet/dry) weather.

B Collect records of your local weather for one week. You may find this in a local newspaper. Try to obtain measurements for rainfall, temperature, day length and hours of sun. Display the measurements in suitable graphs. Was the weather typical for the time of year?

C Make up your own *Wordwise* box of any new words that you have found in this section.

D Look at the information about tides in the *Factfile*. Produce a poster or magazine article explaining why we have tides. Why do you think there are two tides each day and not just one?

E There are many proverbs and sayings about the weather. Collect together some of these and then decide whether or not they are true. Here are some to get you started.

'If the glass falls low, prepare for a blow.'

'When mountains and cliffs in the sky appear,
Some sudden and violent showers are near.'

'Red sky at night, shepherd's delight,
Red sky in the morning, shepherd's warning.'

F You have been asked to set up a weather station in your school grounds. You will need to decide

- where it will go;
- what you are going to measure;
- how you will make the measurements;
- how often you will collect the results; and
- how you will display them.

Produce a report with suitable diagrams which shows your plans for the weather station.

G Make a diary for one month to show the shape and position of the Moon at the same time each evening. Remember you will only be able to see it on clear evenings and when it is in a part of the sky visible from the Earth in darkness.

You will need to show the cloudy evenings when it was not possible to see the Moon. What can you say about the movements of the Moon from your observations?

H Collect newspaper articles and photographs about any severe weather conditions which have had a serious effect on peoples' lives. Make a poster to indicate the problems and discuss any ways of combating such disasters.

The Earth and its climate

Depressing news?

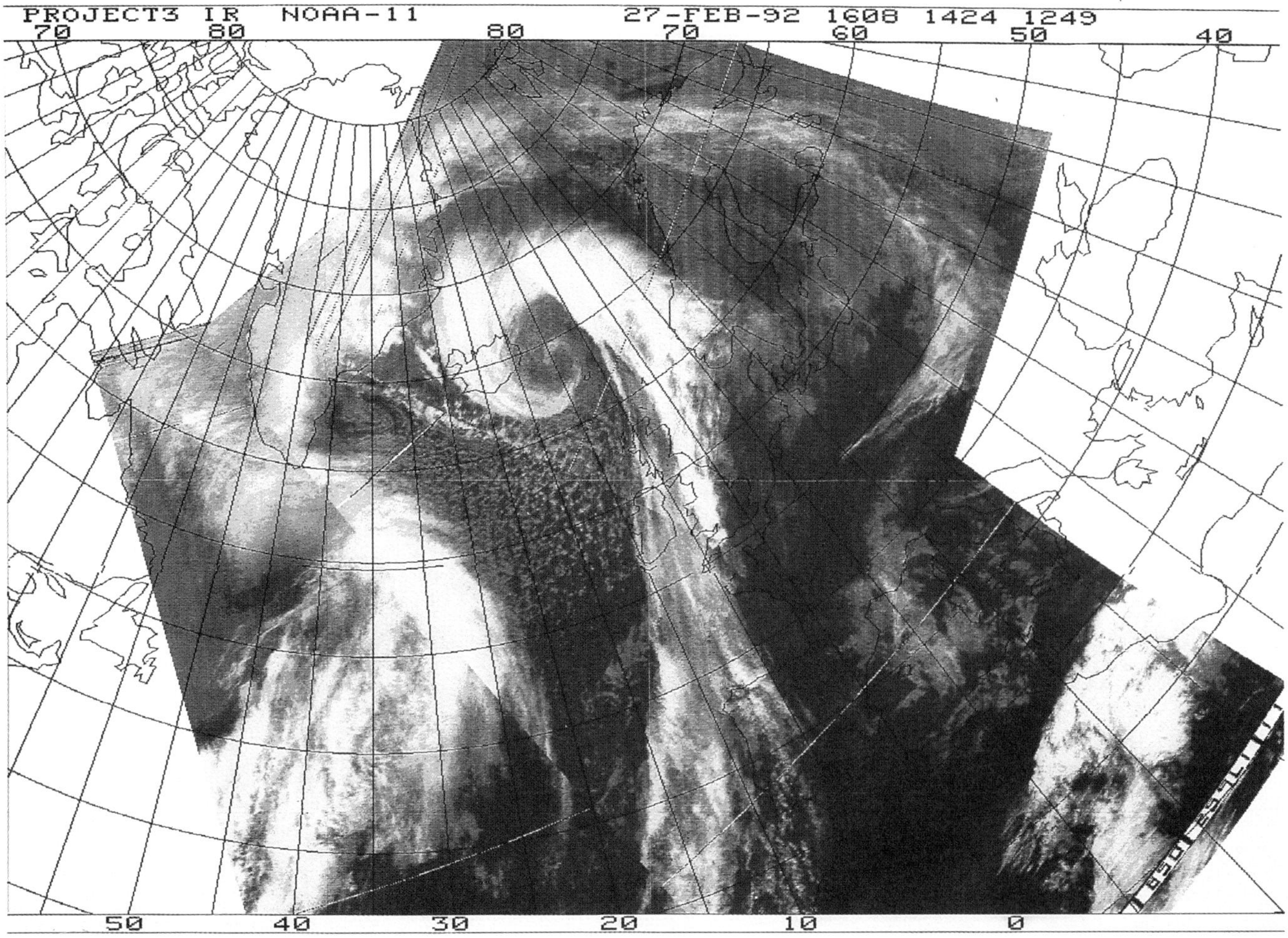

Aerial photograph showing the weather conditions on 27 February 1992.

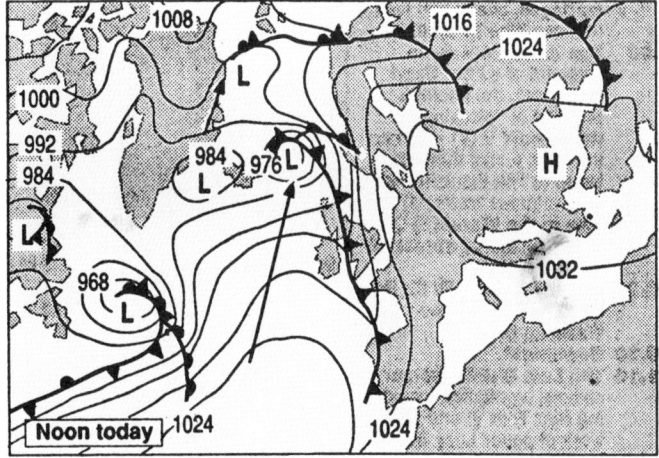

Weather map for 27 February 1992.

a Study the photograph and the weather map of the British Isles for 27 February 1992.

b Use an outline of Britain to produce a simple map to show the expected weather using the symbols in the *Factfile*. Make sure it includes the wind speeds and directions.

c What type of weather would you predict for the next 24 hours?

d Make a tape or a video of your own weather forecast from this information. You will need to produce suitable display material to illustrate your programme.

The solar system

Eclipse!

An eclipse of the Sun happens when the shadow of the Moon falls on to the Earth. In a total eclipse the Sun may seem to be completely blotted out, and it is as dark as night. The next total eclipse that will be visible from Britain will occur on August 11, 1999.

This diagram (not to scale) shows how the Earth orbits the Sun, while the Moon orbits the Earth.

a Redraw the diagram to show the positions during an eclipse of the Sun.
b An eclipse of the Moon occurs when a shadow covers the Moon. What shadow could that be? Change the diagram again to explain how the Moon can be eclipsed.

The 'diamond ring' effect, produced just after a total eclipse of the Sun.

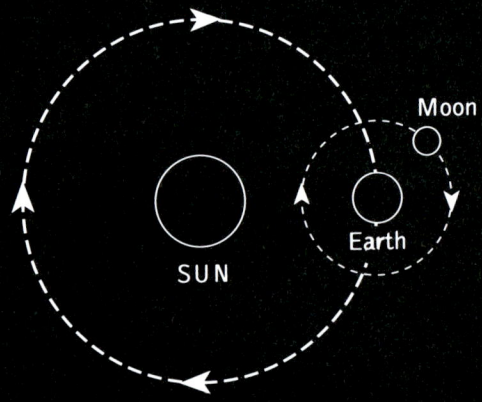

Visual stimulus

The solar system

Mars

Mars is further from the Sun than the Earth, so its average surface temperature is only −23°C. The thin atmosphere is mostly carbon dioxide. The surface is bathed with ultraviolet light from the Sun. This is because there is no ozone layer in the atmosphere. Ozone, which is a form of oxygen, prevents ultraviolet light from reaching the Earth's surface. There is no surface water, although there are features that could be dried up river beds. It is possible that there is ice at the poles. Unmanned spacecraft have landed on Mars but have found no signs of life.

▲ A photograph of Mars taken by the Hubble Space Telescope. White clouds in the Martian atmosphere can be seen on the top left.

◀ A 1976 photograph of the surface of Mars taken by the Viking lander.

Olympus Mons. This extinct volcano is 25 000 m high and covers an area nearly as large as England. ▼

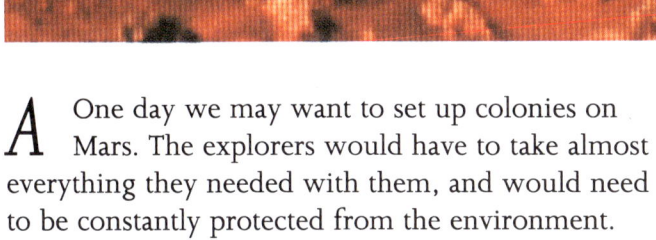

A One day we may want to set up colonies on Mars. The explorers would have to take almost everything they needed with them, and would need to be constantly protected from the environment.
● What features of the planet would give the colonists greatest problems? How would they cope with them? Where would they live? What special clothing and equipment would they need? Why is it important to discover whether there is a store of frozen water on the planet?

B *Viking*'s seismographs found no signs of earthquake activity on Mars, and there are no signs of plate movements such as those causing continental drift on Earth. However, there are extinct volcanoes, so there must have been heat inside the thick crust at some point in the past.
a What signs would you look for on a planet to decide if it had an active core under the crust?
b Research the sizes of Earth's volcanoes and compare them with Olympus Mons. Make scale drawings of them. Discuss possible reasons why Olympus Mons is so much larger than earthly volcanoes.

Visual stimulus

The solar system

> **Key facts: the solar system**
> - The Sun is a star which is 150 million km from the Earth.
> - The Sun's energy comes from **nuclear fusion**. Hydrogen nuclei join to make helium, releasing energy.
> - The Sun and planets were formed from a hot gas cloud called a **nebula**.
> - The composition of the planets depends on how close they are to the Sun. The inner planets have metallic cores and rocky crusts; the outer planets are less dense and made of light elements.
> - The Earth's atmosphere has slowly changed due to photosynthesis by plants producing oxygen and removing carbon dioxide.

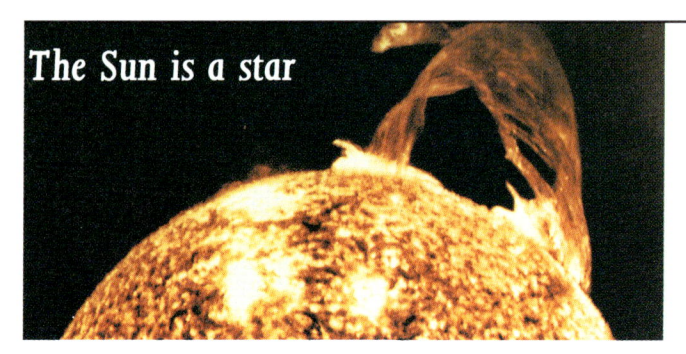

The Sun is a star

The Sun, showing a 'prominence' (an arching plume of hot gas).

The Sun is a star very similar to the others we can see in the night sky. The important difference for us is that the Sun is very much closer: just 150 million km away! The Sun's light takes about 8 minutes to travel from the Sun to the Earth, but the light from the next nearest star takes more than 4 years to reach us. The Sun is very much larger than the Earth. It is 1.4 million km in diameter, compared to the Earth's diameter of 12 756 km. In volume it is over a million times bigger than Earth. It is made mainly of hydrogen (71%) and helium (27%). These gases are extremely hot. On the surface of the Sun the temperature is 6000°C, and the core is at least 14 million °C.

Nuclear fusion. The Sun's energy comes from a process called nuclear fusion, which happens at the very high temperatures found inside the Sun. The nuclei of hydrogen atoms join (fuse) together to make helium. When this happens some of the mass is turned into energy. Because of this the Sun is slowly 'losing weight' and will eventually run out of fuel. We do not need to worry about this, as there is enough left for about another 5000 million years.

The solar system

The Sun has a family of planets in orbit around it. There are nine main planets, including our own Earth. There is also a band of minor planets called the **asteroids**. All the planets orbit the Sun in the same direction.

All the planets' orbits are also in the same *plane* – they move around as if they are on a flat table top, with the Sun in the centre. The planets orbit at different speeds. The nearer they are to the Sun the faster they make one orbit, so they all have different lengths of 'years'.

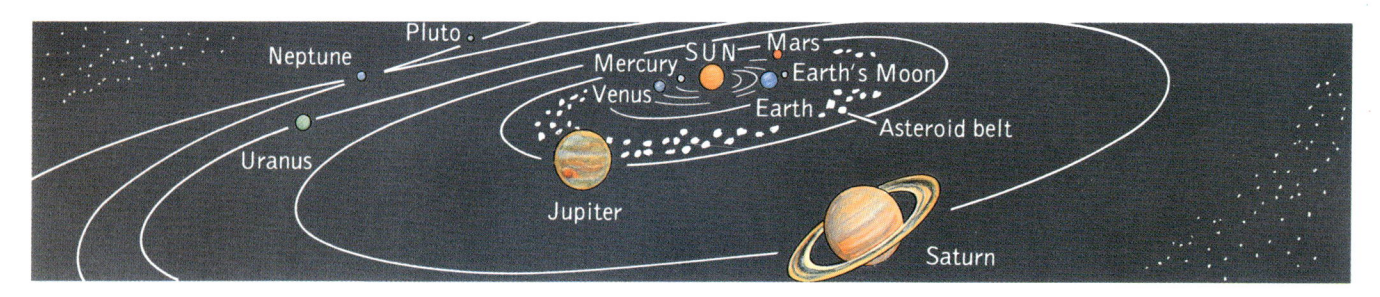

	Mercury	Venus	Earth	Mars	Jupiter	Saturn	Uranus	Neptune	Pluto
Distance from Sun (millions of km)	58	108	150	228	778	1 427	2 870	4 497	5 900
Orbital period (Earth days)	88	225	365	687	4333	10 759	30 685	60 190	90 465

Factfile

The solar system

How the planets were formed

There are several theories about this. Any theory has to fit these facts:
- All the planets' orbits are in the same plane.
- They all go round the Sun in the same direction.
- The inner planets (Mercury, Venus, Earth, Mars) are dense, with metallic cores and rocky crusts.
- The outer planets (Jupiter, Saturn, Uranus and Neptune) are much less dense. They may have small rocky cores, but are mostly made of light elements such as hydrogen.

The solar nebula theory. About 5000 million years ago the Sun and planets were formed from a very hot cloud or **nebula**. It was mostly made of hydrogen and helium, but other elements were there as well. Because of the high temperature (over 2000°C) every element was in the form of a gas. Slowly the cloud cooled, and the gaseous elements

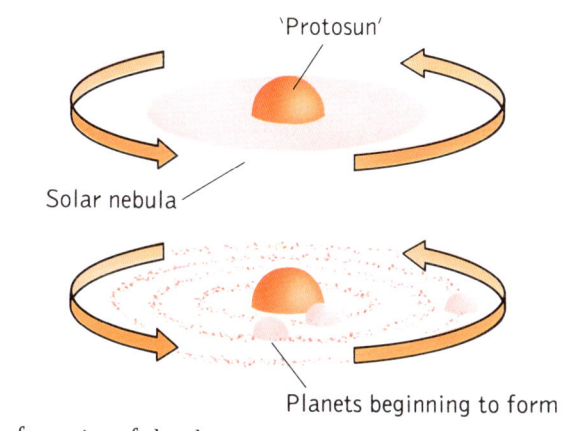

The formation of the planets.

Jupiter, a gas giant. The 'red spot' is believed to be a persistent storm.

began to condense into particles, in the same way that steam condenses into water and then forms ice if it is cold enough. Near the Sun the temperature remained hot, so metal and rocky silicate particles were formed. Further out from the Sun it became much colder, so hydrogen and helium were able to condense. Eventually the particles gathered together to form the planets, all still going in the same direction as the original cloud.

Owing to the temperature differences when they formed, the planets nearer the Sun contained most of the metals and rocks so they, including the Earth, have metal cores and rocky crusts. The outer planets contain very little metal or rock so they have very low densities compared to Earth. They have only small cores and are sometimes called 'gas giants'. They consist mostly of thick atmospheres of hydrogen and chemicals containing a lot of hydrogen, such as methane and ammonia. What we think of as the surfaces of Jupiter and Saturn are not really surfaces at all. Our telescopes are just seeing the top of the atmospheres: there would be nowhere to land a spaceship!

Earth's atmosphere

There are many different gases trapped in the rocks that make up the Earth's crust. Water (H_2O), carbon dioxide (CO_2), nitrogen (N_2), and hydrogen sulphide (H_2S) are all released to this day by volcanoes and hot springs. It is most likely that the Earth's atmosphere consisted of these gases to start with. As the Earth cooled, the water vapour would have become liquid, forming the first seas. This would have left an atmosphere of carbon dioxide and nitrogen. At some point, perhaps about 2900 million years ago, the first simple plants evolved and began to change the atmosphere. Photosynthesis uses energy from the Sun to turn carbon dioxide and water into food. Oxygen is made at the same time. Thanks to these first green plants the atmosphere slowly became the mixture of nitrogen and oxygen (with a little carbon dioxide) that we know today.

Bubbling mud pools and hot springs release gases such as hydrogen sulphide and carbon dioxide into the atmosphere.

Factfile

Pulling together

Newton's theory of gravitation tells us that any two objects are pulled together by the force of gravity – even two people standing near each other have a tiny gravitational force between them. Newton's ideas explain the movement of all the planets around the Sun, and the stars in their galaxies, but he began by thinking just about the Moon.

Newton knew that the force of gravity caused objects to fall towards the centre of the Earth. He wondered whether there might be a force of attraction between the Moon and the Earth. He already had some of the ideas he needed to solve the problem. In his **First Law of Motion** he had set out this idea:

'... a body in motion moves in a straight line unless acted on by a force.'

The Moon is not moving in a straight line; it follows a more or less circular path round the Earth. Therefore there must be some force acting on it, curving its path.

How does the Moon stay in orbit?

If left to itself the Moon would follow Newton's First Law and drift off into space. The tendency of the Moon to move away in a straight line is balanced by the opposing force of gravity pulling the Moon and Earth together. As a result, the distance between the Earth and Moon stays about the same.

Newton thought about it in more detail. He imagined a cannon-ball being fired from a mountain top, parallel to the ground. The force of gravity pulls the ball downwards, so it follows a curved path and eventually hits the ground. The faster we fire the ball, the further it will travel before it lands. Now, the surface of the Earth is also curved. If the firing speed were just enough to make the downward track of the ball match exactly the curve of the Earth, as fast as the ball fell down the surface of the Earth would fall away underneath it. The ball would then never get any closer to the Earth – it would be in orbit. Newton had the idea of an orbiting satellite in the 1660s!

Gravity weakens with distance

Newton knew that the Moon moves at about 1 km/s in its orbit. This is a lot slower than the speed he worked out for his orbiting cannon-ball, which would need a speed of 8 km/s to balance the strong pull of the Earth. The Moon needs less speed to balance the pull of the Earth than the cannon-ball. This told him that the Earth and the Moon attract each other relatively weakly. This is because the Moon is so far away. The further apart two objects are the less strongly they attract each other.

The full theory

Gravity pulls all objects together, not just the Earth and the Moon. The strength of the attraction depends on two things:
- **The mass of the two objects.** The greater the mass of an object, the stronger the attraction. We weigh more on Earth than we would on the Moon because the Earth's greater mass exerts a greater force on us.
- **The distance between the objects.** Gravity weakens with distance. It obeys an *inverse square* law. If the distance between two bodies doubles, the attraction drops to a quarter ($1/2^2$). If the distance goes up by 3 times the gravity drops to one ninth ($1/3^2$).

The force of gravity is proportional to $\frac{M \times m}{d^2}$.

where M and m are the masses of the objects and d is the distance between them.

The faster a cannon-ball is fired, the further it will travel. If you could fire it fast enough, it would go into orbit around the Earth.

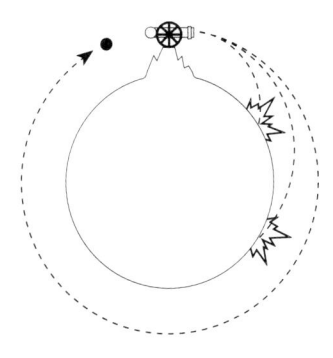

The solar system

Space travel

For Newton's cannon-ball really to stay in orbit it would have to be up above the atmosphere, say about 600 km high. Otherwise, friction with the air would slow it down and make it crash. This means that a launch rocket has two jobs to do. It must lift its satellite high above the atmosphere so that air resistance is not a problem, and then accelerate it to the right speed so it can stay in orbit.

What is the right speed?

Earth's gravity decreases as we go further away from it so the right speed is less as we get higher. Low orbits, such as those used by the space shuttle, need the highest speeds – not much less than Newton's cannon-ball's 8 km/s. Very high orbits need slower speeds. Many communications satellites are placed at a height of 35 000 km. They have to travel at 3 km/s. This particular orbit is very useful, because at that speed the satellite keeps up with the spin of the Earth. It seems to hover over a fixed place on the surface. Such an orbit is said to be **geocentric**. It makes aiming our satellite TV receivers much easier!

Escaping the Earth

If we want to launch a rocket which can leave Earth's gravity altogether and travel to the other planets it must break out of its orbit around the Earth. This means reaching speeds higher than that of Newton's orbiting cannon-ball. To escape the Earth completely a speed of 11 km/s is required. This is called the **escape velocity**. Even this is not enough to get a rocket right out of the solar system to visit other stars. To do that we also have to escape from the Sun's gravity, and that means even more speed.

Reaching these very high speeds is what limits our exploration of space. The problem is to load enough fuel on to a rocket so it can reach the

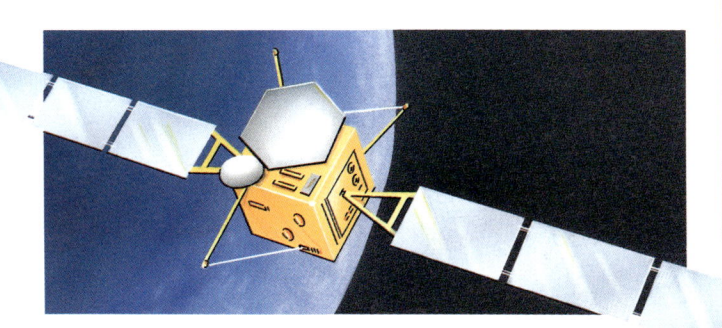

The Space Shuttle. Note how much space is given over to carrying fuel.

necessary speeds, without making it too heavy to fly. Launchers can now be built which give us enough speed, so sending astronauts to the other planets in our solar system is possible. Perhaps you will walk on Mars one day! Exploring other stars will be much more difficult, especially for a human crew. At 40 km/s (the Sun's escape velocity) the journey to the nearest star would take 30 000 years. Even at the speed of light (3×10^8 m/s) it would take over 4 years.

- Find out how fast the Moon moves.
a Observe the Moon moving against the background of the stars. See how many of its own diameters it moves through in one hour.
b Now work out how far the Moon has moved. One diameter is 3480 km.
c Use this formula to calculate the velocity:
$$\text{Velocity} = \frac{\text{distance}}{\text{time}}.$$
If you take 1 hour as the time, your answer will be in kilometres per hour. What is it in kilometres per second?

Background reading

? The solar system

Questions and activities

A Complete this paragraph using words from the list.

**galaxy   hydrogen   nuclear fusion   orbit
planets   stars   universe**

The Sun is mostly made of the gases _____ and helium. It makes energy by a process called _____ _____. This energy provides light and heat for a family of nine _____ which are in _____ around the Sun.

B The *Apollo* missions to the Moon were launched by the 120-m-high *Saturn* rocket. Most of its mass consisted of fuel used in the initial launch. The used rocket was left behind and only a small part – the command module and the lunar excursion module – went on to the Moon. The command module took up an orbit around the Moon; the excursion module left it and went down to the surface. It used its rockets to slow down and land gently. Moving clumsily in the Moon's low gravity the astronauts explored and collected samples. Then they lifted off using the rockets on the excursion module and joined up with the command module. This had its own fuel and engines, and was used to return home. The astronauts 'splashed down' into the sea using parachutes to slow their descent.
a Why did the excursion module need very little fuel to lift off from the Moon, compared to the enormous amounts used by the *Saturn* launcher to leave the Earth?
b What methods were used to control the speed at which the command module landed on the Earth and Moon?

'One small step...'

Sunspots. Many are larger than the Earth.

C It is possible to observe changes on the surface of the Sun although **you must never look directly at it**, either through telescopes and binoculars or with the naked eye: you can easily burn the retina of your eye and be left permanently blind.

If your school has a suitable telescope you can use it to project an image of the Sun on to a screen. The only features you can see for yourself on the surface of the Sun are sunspots. These are dark irregular patches which are cooler than the rest of the surface and are caused by the Sun's magnetic field. They are very large; a small one is larger than the Earth. The number of sunspots varies on an 11-year cycle; there were many in 1990/91, and there will be another maximum in 2002. In between there are fewer, but you should still be able to see some.

Use sunspots to study the rotation of the Sun.
a Use the telescope projector method to make a map of the main sunspots.
b Repeat the experiment every day you can for two weeks. Write the date and time on every map.
c Use your results to work out how long it takes the Sun to make one complete rotation.

Your results will depend on the position of the sunspots. Those near the Sun's equator rotate faster than those near the poles. The Sun 'twists itself up' – it is not a solid object, and the equator rotates quicker than the rest.

A question of scale

Diagrams of the Sun and planets like the one on page 36 are not usually drawn to scale because the sizes and distances make it impossible to show the pictures on a normal page. The distances between the planets are so large that the planets would have to be drawn as tiny dots.

a Make scale drawings of the Sun and planets and cut them out.
b To make the job a little easier you can take the diameters of the planets to the nearest 1000 km.
c Use a scale of 1 cm to 10 000 km.
d Find out the sizes you need to cut by copying and filling in this chart.

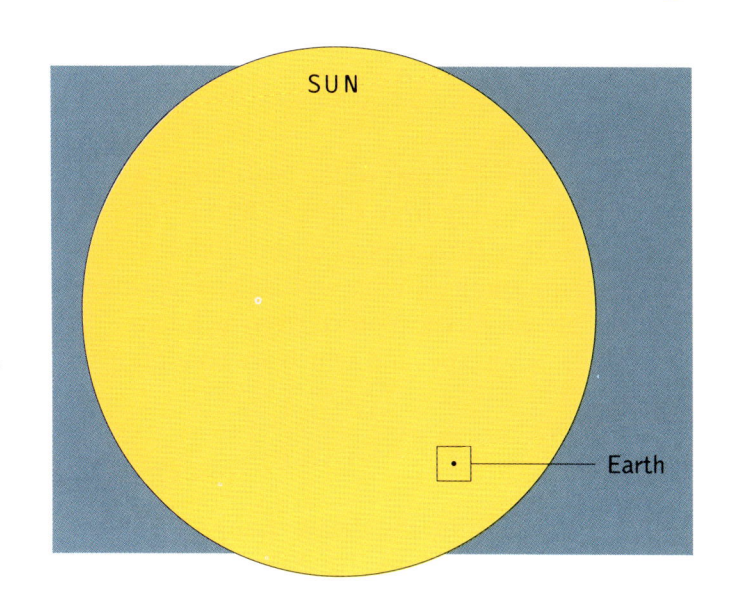

▲ The Sun and Earth shown to scale.

	Actual diameter (km)	Approximate diameter (km) (nearest 1000 km)	Scale diameter (cm) (1 cm ≡ 10 000 km)
Sun	1 392 530	1 393 000	139.3
Mercury	4 878	5 000	0.5
Venus	12 104	12 000	1.2
Earth	12 756		
Mars	6 794		
Asteroids (e.g. Ceres)	1 003		
Jupiter	142 800		
Saturn	120 000		
Uranus	52 400		
Neptune	49 500		
Pluto	2 200		

Now find the scale distances from the Sun using the same scale. You might be able to lay out the first one or two along the corridor of your school. The rest will just have to be marked on a map!

	Distance from Sun (million km)	Scale distance (cm (m)) (1 cm = 10 000 km)
Mercury	58	5 800 (58)
Venus	108	10 800 (108)
Earth	150	15 000 (150)
Mars	228	22 800 (228)
Asteroids	400	40 000 (400)
Jupiter	778	77 800 (778)
Saturn	1427	142 700 (1427)
Uranus	2870	287 000 (2870)
Neptune	4497	449 700 (4497)
Pluto	5900	590 000 (5900)

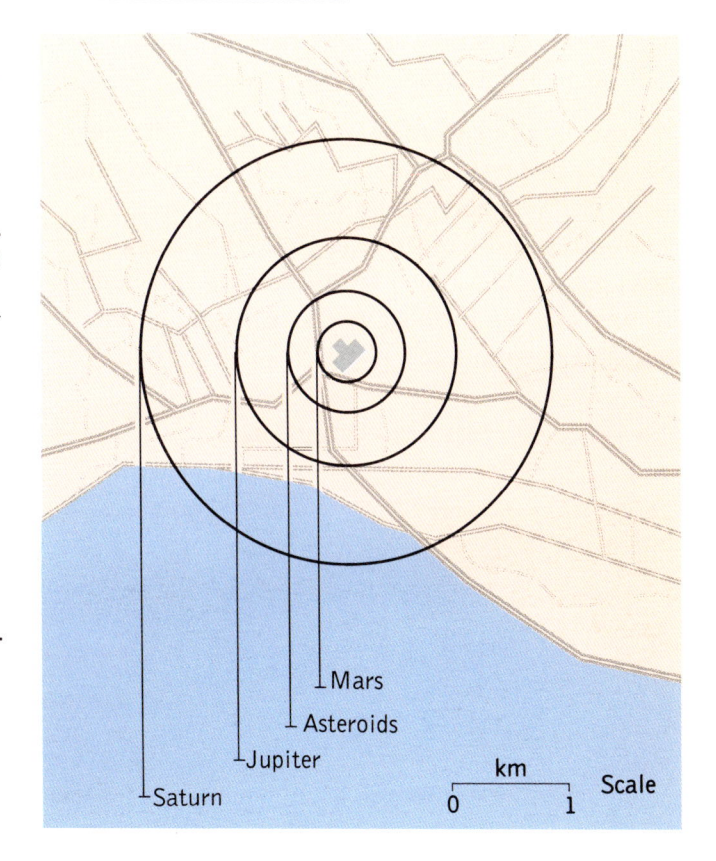

A folded landscape

This is a picture of a part of the coastline of the Isle of Wight, stretching from Culver Cliff to Bembridge. It is fairly typical of the kind of scenery found on the southern coasts of England. A closer look reveals the physical processes which have shaped this landscape, and which are continuing today.

Erosion

The shape of coastlines is always changing as the sea erodes away the shore. How fast the erosion takes place depends on the hardness of the rocks. On this piece of coastline, the Culver Cliff forms the most noticeable feature, standing up taller than the rocks around them, and pushing farther out to sea. This is because they are made of chalk, which is much harder than the sandstone and clay that surround it. Erosion by the sea affects the chalk less.

Folding

The cliff faces show layers or **strata** which are nearly vertical, although in places they dip at a gentler angle. But the rocks on this part of the coast are all sedimentary, and were laid down as horizontal layers on a sea bed. How did they come to be at such an angle?

We usually think of rocks as hard. But when they are subjected to high pressures, they become much more pliable, bending and folding over on themselves. If the pressure is great, they can also form great cracks called **faults**. Folding and faulting occur when the Earth's crust is deformed by the collision of continental plates.

Culver Cliff, Isle of Wight.

The layers of sedimentary rock making up this coastline started off horizontal but were tipped up by earth movements which were also, far away, producing the Alps. This happened over 25 million years ago. Over the years, erosion has exposed the vertical layers and laid out a time sequence of older and older strata horizontally.

Walking back in time...

Walking along the coast from the northern end of the bay near Bembridge to Culver Cliff is like taking a journey back in time. We can tell under what conditions each layer of rock was laid down by clues left in the rock. This part of the Isle of Wight was underwater for many millions of years. The rocks are made of sediments and fossils deposited in water. Here is what we would find if we started off from the point marked X on the map and continued southwards.

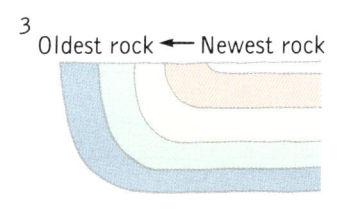

How folding and erosion creates vertical strata.

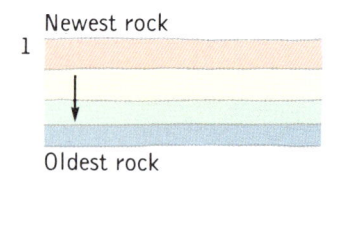

1. Newest rock / Oldest rock — Original horizontal beds of rock
2. Folding tips the rock
3. Oldest rock ← Newest rock — Erosion levels the surface

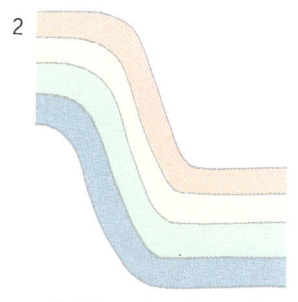

Case study 1

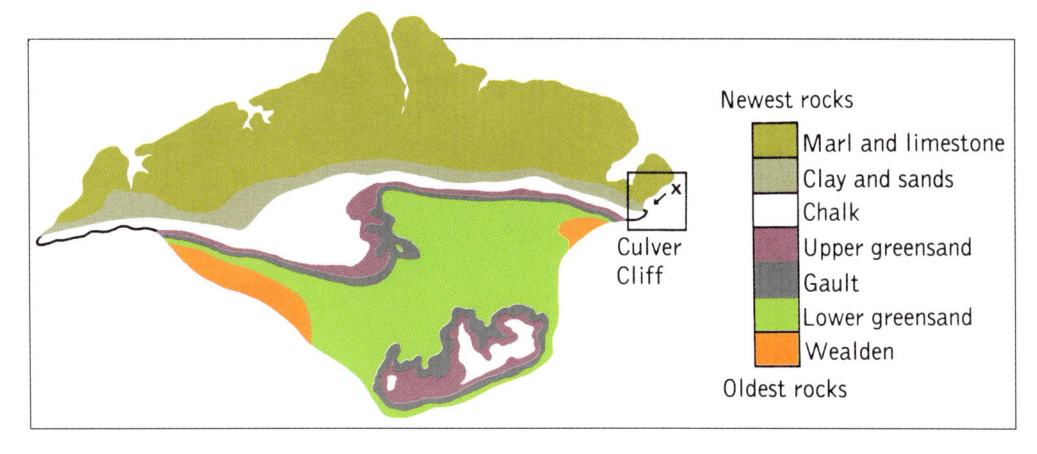

A folded landscape

The Isle of Wight.

A river estuary.

Sand dunes.

A belemnite.

Bembridge Limestone: 40 million years ago
These are the youngest rocks in our sequence. Limestone is calcium carbonate, and consists of the remains of the shells of tiny marine creatures. In the Bembridge limestone we find fossils of fresh water snails and sometimes even land snails. At one time a river ran into the sea here forming an estuary, where layers of dead marine organisms built up on the bottom.

Bracklesham Beds: 50 million years ago
This layer is a layer of dark grey clay. It contains fossils of marine molluscs, so the clay must have settled on the bed of an ancient, slow-moving sea.

Bagshot Sands: 60 million years ago
This layer of coloured sandstone contains no fossils of sea creatures so the original sands may not have been on the bed of a sea. Perhaps this was once an area of sand dunes formed from particles blown along by the wind, or the beach of a shallow sea.

Culver Cliff: 120 million years ago
These are made of the oldest rocks in our sample. Chalk is another form of calcium carbonate (see also Section 2), so these rocks too are made of the remains of sea shells. We find here the fossils of ancient sea creatures such as *belemnites* and *ammonites*. When these rocks were being formed the area was covered with a sea.

A Investigate what physical processes may have shaped the area in which you live. Your teacher will be able to find a geological survey map which will tell you about the rocks in the area. Write an article like this one, based on your research, to show how your area has changed over the years.

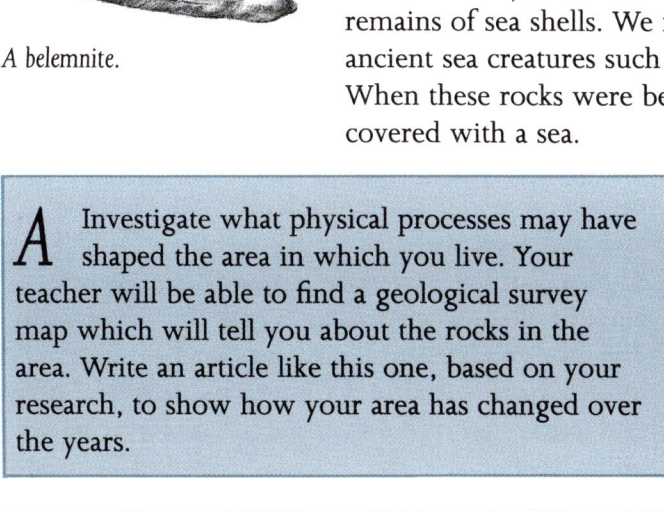

B Find out more about fossil belemnites and ammonites. When did they live? What did they look like? What did they feed on? Do they have any modern living relatives? Look in the geology section of your library or in books about evolution.

Case study 1

Eruption

Volcanoes occur where molten magma and hot gas escape through the Earth's crust. Although we usually think of volcanic eruptions as being huge and dramatic explosions, this is not always true. Sometimes the magma seeps out quite slowly, and new igneous rock is formed without the explosive damage that makes such an impression on us. In other cases there is a tremendous explosion, when the energy in the hot magma and compressed gas is released all at once. To understand why some eruptions are so explosive we need to look at the events that happen inside a volcano. We shall study two particularly impressive eruptions in history: Krakatoa (1883) and Mount St Helens (1980).

Krakatoa

Krakatoa was an island between Sumatra and Java in Indonesia. In August 1883, after three months of explosions that could themselves be heard 150 km away, there were four colossal explosions which could be heard half way round the world. People nearly 5000 km away thought they were hearing cannons firing. The island of Krakatoa was totally destroyed. A column of ash rose to 80 km, almost to the edge of the atmosphere, and produced spectacular sunsets all over the world. A tidal wave which rose to 30 m above sea level swamped low parts of Sumatra and Java, killing 36 000 people.

Inside a volcano.

The island has begun to grow again.

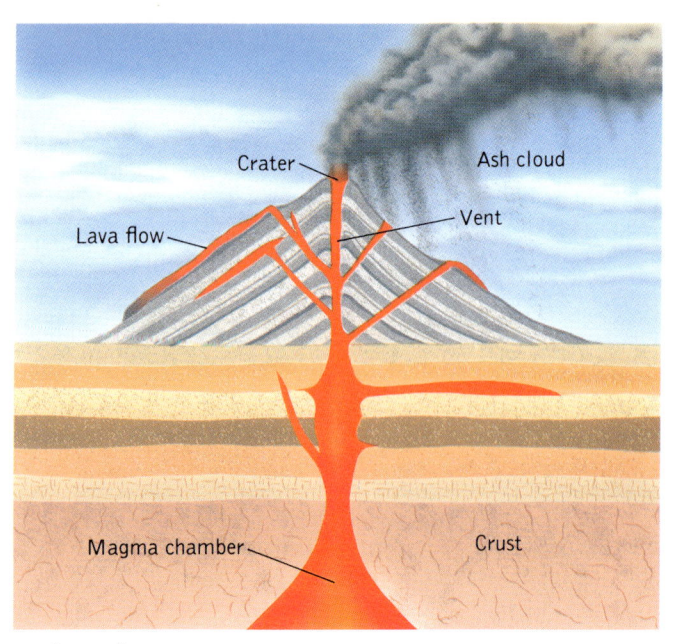

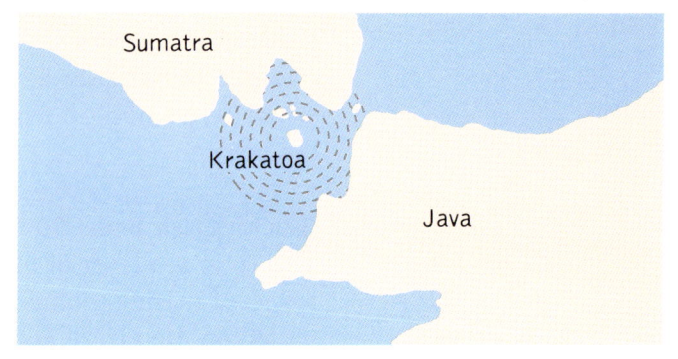

Why was the explosion so powerful? The answer lies in the interaction between the heat of the magma and water. In the early weeks of the eruption the smaller explosions were caused when the steadily rising magma heated up water which was soaked into the porous rocks of the island. Normally water boils to steam at 100°C, but the pressure underground raises the boiling point, so that the water can reach about 200°C without turning to steam. When a crack to the surface opened the pressure was suddenly released, and the superheated water turned to steam all at once. This is known as a **phreatic** explosion. Such minor explosions gave the first signals of the disaster to come. The explosions also set off a chain reaction. They blasted the first cracks open a little wider, and sea water began to seep into the volcano. This caused more explosions, each one making larger and larger openings for water to enter. Finally, in August, the cracks were so large that a massive amount of seawater gushed in and met the magma. The resulting 'steam bomb' created an explosion greater than many atomic bombs put together. It is said to have produced the loudest noise ever heard on the Earth.

Eruption

Mt St Helens, 18 May 1980. After the eruption, 400 m were missing from the summit.

Mount St Helens

In the West of the USA is a mountain range known as the Cascades. One of its most beautiful peaks was Mount St Helens. The snow-capped mountain, surrounded by pine forest, was known to be volcanic, but it had been dormant for over 100 years.

First warnings

In March 1980, minor earth tremors were felt. The volcano was showing the first signs of coming back to life. Later in that month phreatic explosions began, caused by hot rising magma turning the water soaked into the volcano into steam. Such explosions had also marked the beginning of the Krakatoa eruption. They were enough to make a new crater form in the top of the volcano, and served as a warning for the authorities who issued a 'hazard alert'. People were moved out of the area as a precaution.

Pressure builds up

In April and May a huge bulge appeared on the side of the mountain; it grew until it was pushing out 150 m, covering an area 2 km wide. This was a clear sign that a large amount of magma had risen up inside the mountain and had caused the mountain to swell.

Explosion

On May 18 the eruption came to a sudden climax. An earthquake occurred, shaking the bulge loose in a landslide. The pressure that had been containing the magma was suddenly released and tonnes of hot water vaporized in an instant. The same drop in pressure allowed gases such as sulphur dioxide, which had been dissolved in the sticky magma, to turn into bubbles of gas. We see something like this when we open a shaken up can of lemonade: it all gushes out at once when the pressure is let off. Many tonnes of magma and old rock were smashed to tiny pieces of ash which were blasted out sideways faster than a hurricane. At the same time another explosion blew off the top of the mountain, sending even more ash soaring into the sky.

Aftermath

In the explosions, the mountain lost 400 m from its summit. The sideways blast and the later mudflows destroyed trees and property for miles around. One billion pounds worth of damage was caused, and 61 people lost their lives. A column of ash rose 19 km into the sky; when it finally came down again buildings collapsed under its weight, and some dust fell 4000 km away. The summer was poor as far away as England, because of the layer of ash in the atmosphere.

We have seen that volcanoes erupt explosively because of several factors:

- The sudden formation of steam when groundwater meets the hot magma.
- Sea water rushing into the magma: again we have a 'steam bomb'.
- A sudden release of pressure allowing gases dissolved in the magma to come out of solution in a violent way.

Sometimes the magma rises and escapes more gradually, and there is a lava flow without an explosion. This can be just as dangerous. Find out more about this kind of eruption. Make a start by studying Kilauea in Hawaii and Mount Etna in Sicily. Try to discover what it is about their structure that lets them erupt without massive explosions.

Case study 2

The dynamic Universe

Our present view of the Universe is only one of many that people have formed over the centuries. In the West, the Universe was thought of as fairly young (about 6000 years old) and unchanging. This idea lasted until the 17th century. Eastern philosophies were based on the idea of repeated cycles of creation and destruction stretching over millions of years. Almost all cultures gave the Earth a central place in the Universe. As science has developed, however, the view of the scale of the Universe and our place in it have changed dramatically. Nothing, it seems, is permanent.

The changing stars

The Earth and other planets of the solar system are in orbit around a fairly small yellow star we call the Sun. It is one among many millions of stars making up a huge spiral **galaxy**. The Sun and other stars revolve around the centre of the galaxy.

The sky may seem unchanging, but we now know that stars are not permanent. A typical star, like the Sun, is born when a cloud of gas called a **nebula** collapses under its own gravity, heating up as it shrinks until nuclear reactions start in the core. Hydrogen turns to helium, releasing energy and stopping the collapse.

This medieval illustration shows the Earth at the centre of the Universe, surrounded by the Sun, planets and stars.

The star shines until it runs out of hydrogen fuel. The core then contracts until a new nuclear reaction starts: helium changes to carbon. The sudden new release of energy causes the star's outer layers to bloat out, making the star a huge, cool **red giant**. Eventually, the outer layers are puffed off into space leaving the hot dense core. This **white dwarf** goes through various nuclear reactions until no more are possible and it cools to form a black dwarf. In the case of the Sun, this cycle will take about 10 thousand million years.

More massive stars go through this cycle much more quickly and the collapse into a white dwarf is more dramatic: the star explodes as a **supernova**. A tiny, extremely dense core is left. In the case of very massive stars, the gravity around the core is so strong that not even light can escape: the star becomes a **black hole**, so called because it cannot be seen.

Changing galaxies

The Universe contains many thousands of galaxies, often found in groups separated by enormous distances. The most distant galaxies observed are

*The Crab Nebula is the remains of a supernova. At the centre is the dense core of the star which has formed a **pulsar**, emitting radio waves.*

The dynamic Universe

The spiral galaxy in Andromeda.

over 10 000 million light years away! They are not all spiral in shape: many are rounded or irregular. Galaxies too can often be active, hurling out jets of matter and colliding with each other.

The changing Universe

The spectra of light from almost all galaxies appear to be red-shifted by the Doppler effect (see box), indicating that the galaxies must be rushing away from us in every direction. The more distant they are, the faster they are moving. Scientists therefore believe that the Universe is expanding.

The 'Big Bang' theory suggests that the Universe began with an enormous explosion which occurred about 16 billion years ago which hurled matter outwards in all directions. The galaxies we see today are still hurtling outwards from the force of the explosion.

Light years

The distances in astronomy are vast and are usually given in **light years**. A light year is the distance light travels in a year – at a speed of 3×10^8 m/s, this is 9.46 million, million km. The Sun is about 8 light minutes away; the next nearest star over 4 light years away!

The Doppler effect

The siren of a police car or an ambulance appears to become higher as it approaches and to drop in pitch as it travels past. This *apparent* change in frequency is called the **Doppler effect**. The corresponding behaviour in the case of light waves is a change in colour: An approaching object seems to have a spectrum that is shifted towards the blue end (known as blue shift) and a receding one to have a spectrum that is shifted towards the red (red shift). These changes in colour only become noticeable at very high velocities. Almost all galaxies show a red shift.

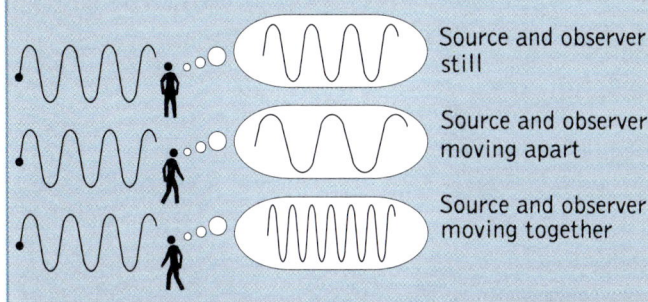

Source and observer still

Source and observer moving apart

Source and observer moving together

The change in pitch is caused by the sound waves seeming to get closer together (higher in frequency) as they reach our ears from an object moving towards us and further apart (lower in frequency) as it moves away.

How will it all end?

There are two main possibilities:

● If the galaxies are moving fast enough to escape their gravitational attraction for each other they will carry on hurtling outwards. Eventually, all the nuclear fuel will run out and the Universe will end up cold and dark.

● If the galaxies have not reached escape velocity, gravitational attraction will slow them down until they stop flying outwards and begin to contract again, perhaps until they come together for another Big Bang. This may have happened many times before!

Which of these two scenarios will it be? The deciding factor is the total mass of the Universe, which would tell us the escape velocity. Scientists are trying to estimate this mass but, so far, the ultimate fate of the Universe remains unknown…

Case study 3

Japan: a disaster waiting to happen

Japan consists of a group of volcanic islands which have grown up near a **convergence zone**. The Pacific Ocean plate is being forced (or **subducted**) under the Asian Plate and is moving under Japan at a rate of 6 cm/year. Most of the population of 122 million live in the coastal plains and Tokyo alone houses almost 20 million people. These people are living on top of an earthquake zone, threatened by volcanoes and tidal waves. Many tiny earth tremors occur every day, but most of them go unnoticed. Occasionally, a major earthquake strikes.

Tokyo 1923: the great Kanto earthquake

At two minutes to noon on September 1st, 1923, the first powerful tremor struck. It was quickly followed by two more major shocks and 171 aftershocks. Ten thousand houses were destroyed and overturned cooking stoves started fires which burnt down three-quarters of the city. Near the coast, further damage was done by a tidal wave 10 m high. The destruction was like that caused by an atom bomb: 140 000 people lost their lives.

Can it happen again?

The historical record suggests that major earthquakes occur in the Tokyo area every 70 years or so. If the pattern still holds, a major disaster could be imminent. There are indications that earthquake activity is building up, with increasing numbers of minor tremors being detected.

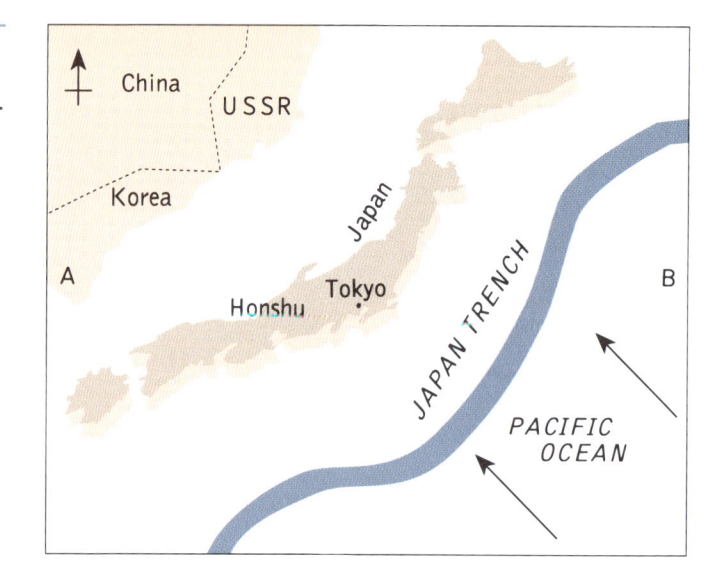

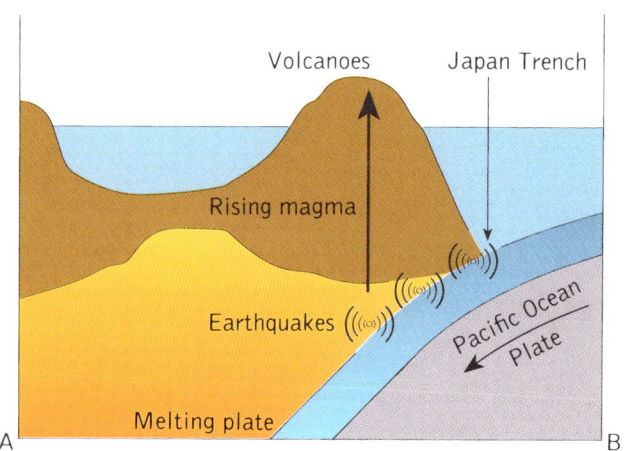

Today, the city is better prepared. All modern buildings are designed to withstand earthquakes. But the population is ten times that in 1923, and Tokyo is a busy urban centre with streets choked with traffic and a maze of flyovers and tunnels carrying high-speed trains. Tokyo also houses the head offices of some of the world's most powerful firms, such as Sony, Toyota and Mitsubishi. If the next earthquake causes as much devastation as in 1923, the bill for reconstruction could reach $847 billion, and the financial repercussions would seriously damage the world economy.

Tokyo today.

Why do earthquakes happen?

Earthquakes occur at the edges of moving tectonic plates. Friction often causes the plates to stick. Eventually, the forces pushing the plates against each other overcome the friction and the plates suddenly slip. This jolting movement, releasing strain energy as heat and seismic waves, is experienced on the surface as an earthquake.

Earthquakes produce three types of **seismic waves**. The **L-waves**, which travel over the Earth's surface, cause the most damage. **P-** and **S-waves** travel through the Earth and are called **body** waves. They can tell us more about the Earth's structure.

The most destructive earthquakes, like those in Japan, occur at subduction zones, where one plate slides under another. Such earthquakes begin deep underground. Earthquakes also occur at the mid-oceanic ridges where plates are moving apart. The new crust here is thin and the earthquakes are usually not very powerful. On the West coast of America, two plates are sliding against each other along a massive fault line, the San Andreas Fault.

The Richter scale

The *strength* of an earthquake is given by a number on the **Richter scale**. This is based on the amount of energy released. The strongest earthquakes are between magnitude 8 and 9. The **Mercalli scale** gives the *intensity* of an earthquake and is based on the damage that occurs.

Mercalli's scale of earthquake intensity	Richter scale of earthquake magnitude
I Recorded only by instruments	3
V Sleepers are woken up. Liquids spill	4.8
VII Difficult to stand. Walls crack and plaster falls	6
X Cracks appear in the ground. Buildings destroyed	7
XII Total destruction. Ground distorted; large landslides	8.1 (maximum known is 8.9)

Extracts from the Richter and Mercalli scales.

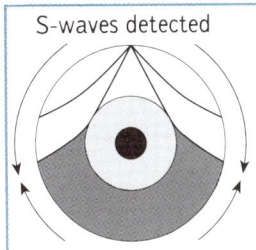

S-waves do not travel through liquids. The large shadow zone shows that the Earth's core must have a liquid outer layer which blocks these waves

P-waves can pass through the liquid layer but are focused *(refracted)* by the core as they pass through, leaving small shadow zones. To act as a lens for P-waves, the core must have a solid centre.

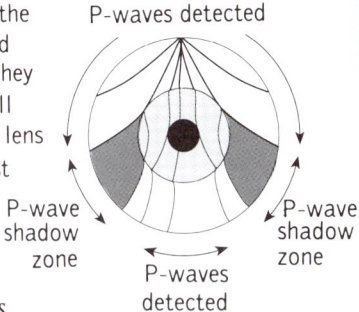

The paths of P- and S-waves.

Predicting earthquakes

Most deaths from earthquakes are caused by buildings falling on people. If an accurate warning could be given, many lives could be saved simply by getting people away from buildings on time. One way to predict earthquakes is to use a **seismograph**. This measures earth movements and can pick up the tiny tremors that often occur before a major earthquake strikes. Unfortunately, much more work needs to be done to make the method reliable.

A Put yourself in the place of a newspaper reporter after the next Tokyo earthquake. Write a report to send back to your newspaper in Europe.

• What are the effects of the earthquake?
• How will the rest of the world be affected in the days to come?

Include a separate scientific piece explaining the cause of the disaster.

B The Armenian earthquake of 1988 devastated whole villages, killing people and making tens of thousands homeless. The earthquake that struck San Francisco in 1989 killed only 63 people. Both measured 6.9 on the Richter scale. Why were the effects of the two earthquakes so different?

Bode's rule

In Section 5 we saw how Newton started with some information about the movement of the Moon and built it up to the theory of gravity. Science often works like that. We begin with simple observations. We collect information, name objects and classify them into groups, and take measurements. Gradually we build up a picture of nature, and we start looking for patterns to help us understand it better. Finally we may come up with a complete theory which tries to explain our observations. Sometimes it can take hundreds of years to find the reasons for the things we have observed. Every generation of scientists builds on the discoveries of those who went before. A typical example of a really long investigation is that of the distances of the planets from the Sun.

The first scientist?

Observing

By the middle of the 17th Century most of the planets had been discovered, and their distances from the Sun were known. This diagram shows what was known at that time. The distances from the Sun are drawn to scale.

The average distance from the Earth to the Sun is 149 600 000 km. It is easier to call this distance one **Astronomical Unit** (AU). Measuring all the planetary distances in astronomical units allows us to work with simple numbers.

Johann Bode.

Planet	Distance from Sun (AU)
Mercury	0.39
Venus	0.72
Earth	1.0
Mars	1.52
Jupiter	5.2
Saturn	9.58

Looking for a pattern

We can see that the gap between each planet widens out as we go away from the Sun. In 1772 two German astronomers, Bode and Titus, looked to see if there was a mathematical pattern to the numbers. After many attempts, they came up with this simple series:

Step 1 Doubling	0	3	6	12	24	48	96
Step 2 Adding 4	4	7	10	16	28	52	100
Step 3 Divide by 10	**0.4**	**0.7**	**1.0**	**1.6**	**2.8**	**5.2**	**10.0**

(Bode number)

If these numbers are compared with the distances from the Sun of the planets that were then known, the result is surprising:

Planet	Distance from Sun (AU)	Bode number
Mercury	0.39	0.4
Venus	0.72	0.7
Earth	1.0	1.0
Mars	1.52	1.6
		2.8
Jupiter	5.2	5.2
Saturn	9.58	10.0

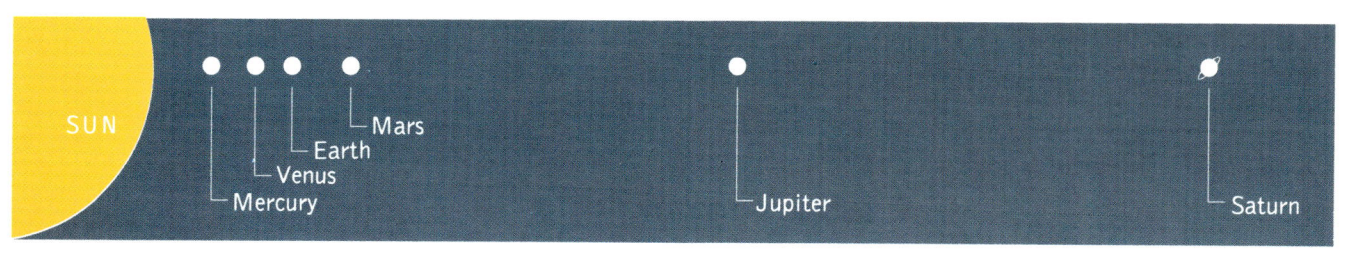

Saturn, as seen by the Voyager spacecraft.

Testing the rule

Not only did the Bode–Titus mathematical series fit the distances very closely, but it suggested a way of testing the rule. Was there another planet to be discovered at 2.8 AU from the Sun? Astronomers all over the world began to search the skies. In 1801 they were successful. A small planet called Ceres was discovered in just the right place. Soon many other small bodies were found at a similar distance, and it was realized that the gap between Mars and Jupiter was filled not by one planet, but by many small ones, which we now call the Asteroids. The pattern has passed an important test: It has been used to make a successful prediction.

Explaining

The exact meaning of this remarkable fit is still not fully understood well over 200 years later. Why should the planets be arranged in such a neat pattern? The answer must lie in the way the planets were formed from the solar nebula (see page 39). Bode's rule will play its part in helping us to understand more about the way the Earth and all the planets came into being.

The Bode formula

We do not have to build up the Bode series by filling in the columns one by one. The whole idea can be set out in one mathematical formula. Then you can use it to find the Bode number for any planet you like without having to do all of the others.

$$d = 0.4 + 0.3 \, (2^n)$$

where d is the Bode number and n is a number given to each planet working outwards from the Sun. We call Venus 0, Earth 1, Mars 2, Asteroids 3, and so on. The formula breaks down for Mercury.

As an example, for Mars, $n = 2$, so

$$\begin{aligned} d &= 0.4 + 0.3 \, (2^2) \\ &= 0.4 + 0.3 \, (4) \\ &= 0.4 + 1.2 \\ &= 1.6 \end{aligned}$$

The formula gives us a Bode number of 1.6 for Mars.

Since Bode's day more planets have been discovered. Their distances are not quite so easy to fit into the series. Things may not be quite so simple as we thought!

- Copy out the Bode series chart set out above. Give it three more columns. Work out the Bode number for those extra columns. That will give you the predicted distances for the next three planets, which Bode did not know about. Here are their actual distances from the Sun:

Uranus   19.2 AU
Neptune   30.1 AU
Pluto   39.5 AU

- Try to match up these distances with the Bode series. How good is the match for each planet? Can you find a better match by putting planets into the 'wrong' column?

Neptune: a challenge for Bode?

The night sky

For many centuries, the only clues we had about our place in the Universe came from observing the night sky. To ancient peoples, the patterns of the stars resembled gods and goddesses, heroes and heroines, and many animals. Many of the constellations are named after characters from Greek and Roman mythology.

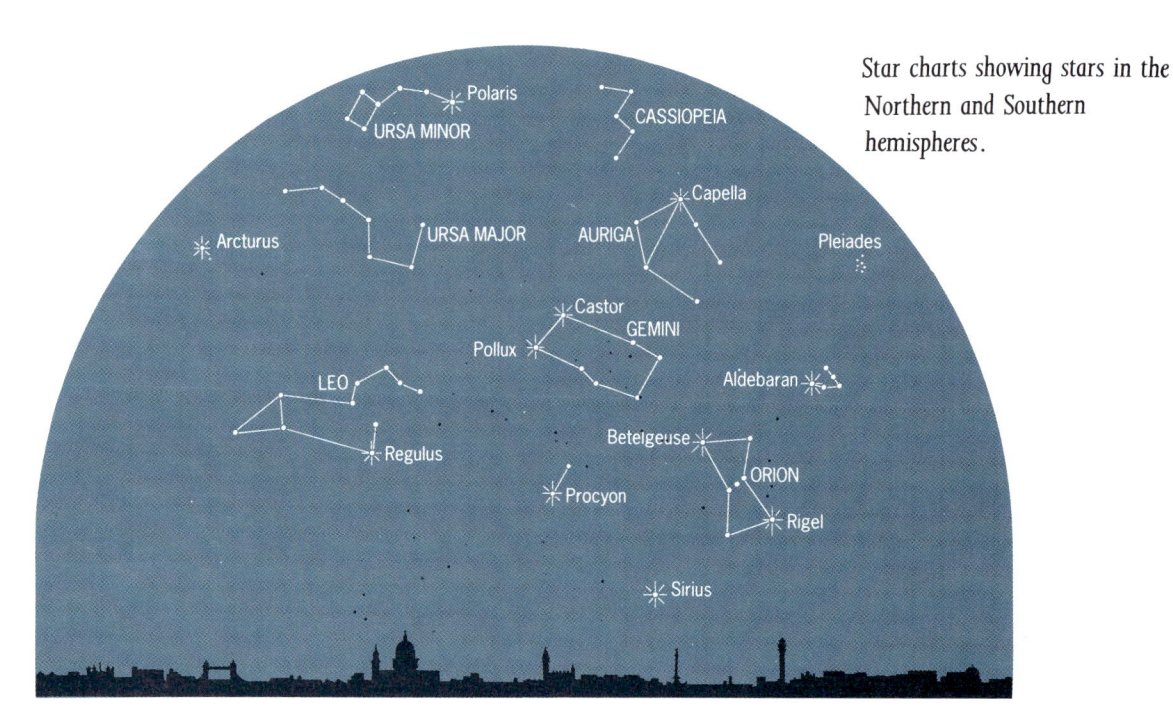

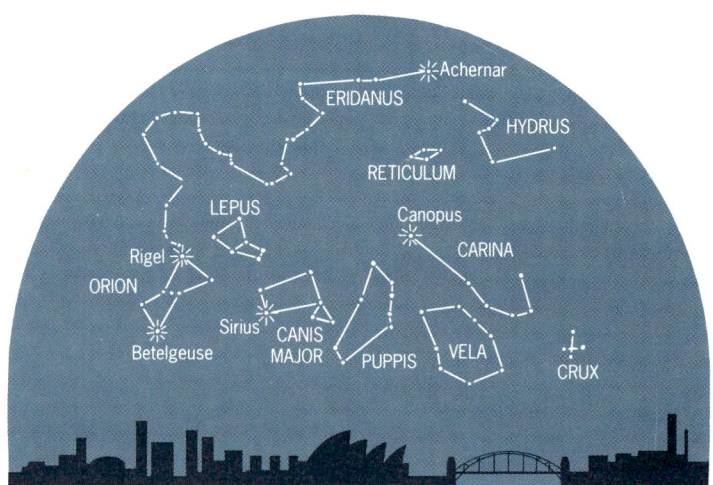

Star charts showing stars in the Northern and Southern hemispheres.

From Australia many of the constellations visible in the north can also be seen. There are also many that cannot be seen at all from England. One example is the Southern Cross.

The night sky

A time exposure shows how the Earth's spinning makes the stars appear to move.

If we observe the northern sky we see that the stars move across the sky during the night. In fact they all appear to move in circles around a star called Polaris, the Pole Star. Stars very close to Polaris make complete circles, so they are called circumpolar stars. For stars further away we only see part of their circle when they rise above the horizon and move across the sky before setting. It is not, of course, the stars that are moving round the Earth, but the Earth that is spinning on its axis, making the stars appear to move. Polaris is directly above the North Pole, so the other stars seem to wheel round it.

If you can see Polaris, you can find directions without a compass. How high Polaris appears in the sky depends on your latitude: at the North Pole it is directly overhead and at the Equator, it is on the horizon. To find the pole star, look for the 'Plough', a part of the constellation of Ursa Major. Two of the stars, the 'pointers', lead the eye to Polaris.

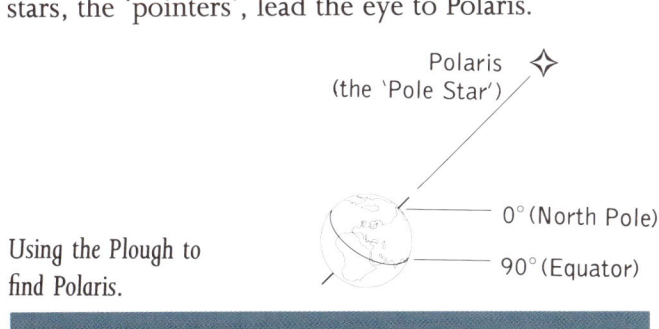

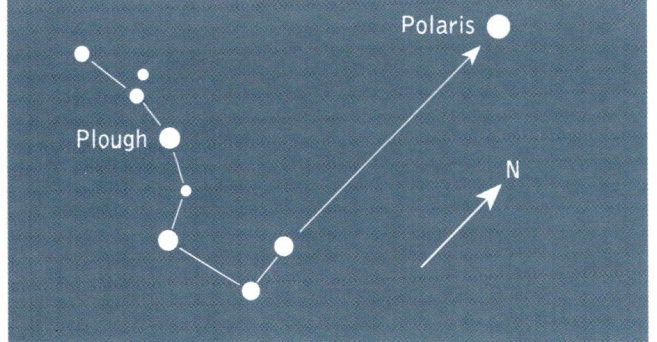

Using the Plough to find Polaris.

Polaris (the 'Pole Star')
0° (North Pole)
90° (Equator)

Polaris
Plough
N

Looking beyond the stars

Our Sun is situated towards the rim of a flat, spiral-shaped galaxy. When we look towards the centre of the spiral, the many distant stars merge to appear as a pale band of light called the Milky Way.

If you live away from city lights, you can just make out a near neighbour, the large spiral galaxy in the constellation of Andromeda, as a faint blur. This is the furthest object you can see with the naked eye: it is 2 million light years away.

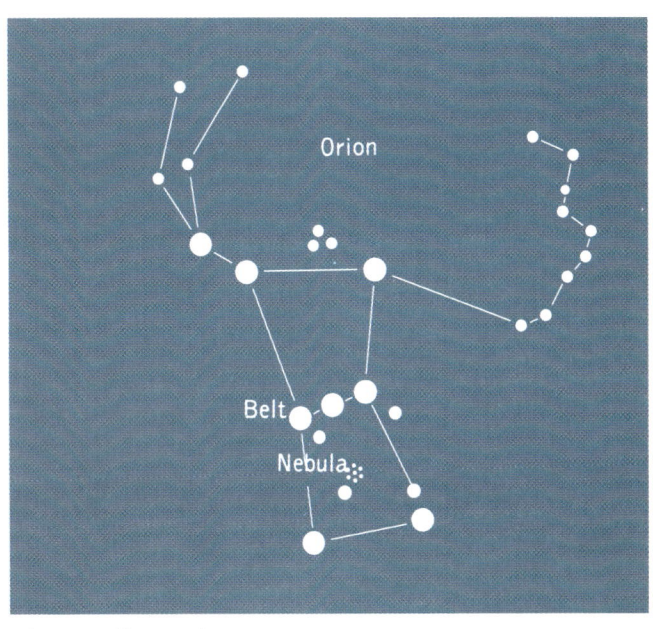

Orion
Belt
Nebula

The constellation of Orion.

- Make your own observations of the sky. Use binoculars or a telescope if you have them – they will not make the stars seem any larger but you will see many more of the fainter ones. You will also see more if you are away from street lighting.

You will notice that different stars are visible at different times of year, although from England you can always see the circumpolar stars.

To start with, look for these things:
- The 'Plough'.
- The Pole Star (Polaris).
- The Milky Way.
- Orion (the hunter). Find the three stars in his belt. Below that, in his sword, is a distant nebula, a huge cloud of gas and dust where new stars are being formed.
- On a really clear night, the Andromeda galaxy.
- Your own star sign – all the signs of the zodiac are constellations.

Extension pages

Index

Andromeda galaxy 55
Aral Sea 25
Asteroids 53
Atlantic Ocean 9, 11
acid rain 22, 23
air pressure 31, 32
ammonite 15, 16, 45
anticyclone 31
aquifer 22
atmosphere 38, 39

Bode's rule 52
basalt 14, 16
belemnite 45
big bang theory 49
black hole 48
building materials 21, 23

Ceres 53
calcium carbonate 16, 17, 23, 45
carbon dioxide 38
cementation 14
chalk 16, 44
clay 24, 45
climate 17, 30, 33
coccoliths 16
cold front 31
compaction 14
condensation 22
constellation 55
continental drift 6, 7, 17
convergence zone 7, 50
core 4, 6, 39
crust 4, 6, 7, 8
cyclone 31

dating rocks 15
deposition 14
depression 31, 33
divergence zone 7
Doppler effect 49

Earth 28, 30, 38, 39, 48, 52
earthquake 5, 6, 7, 9, 50, 51
eclipse of Moon 36
eclipse of Sun 36
equator 28, 30, 55
erosion 12, 14, 44
escape velocity 41
evaporation 22, 25

faulting 5, 7, 44
flint 16
fluorite 23
folding 5, 7, 44
formation of planets 39
fossils 14, 15, 16, 17

galaxy 48, 49
geological timescale 15
granite 14, 16, 23
gravity 30, 40, 41

hurricane 32

L-wave 51
lakes 20
lava 6
light year 49
limestone 14, 17, 22, 23, 45

Marianas Trench 9
Mars 37, 39, 41, 52, 53
Mercalli scale 51
Mercury 39, 52
Milky Way 55
Moon 30, 36, 40, 41
Mount St Helens 46, 47
magma 4, 6, 7, 8, 14, 16, 46, 47
mantle 4, 7, 8
marble 14, 16, 17
metamorphic rock 8, 14, 16, 23
mid-ocean ridge 6, 9
molluscs 16, 45
mountain building 5, 8

Neptune 39, 53
North Pole 28, 55
nebula 38, 39
nuclear fusion 38, 48

Orion 54, 55
ocean trench 7, 9
orbit 30, 39, 41
oxygen 38
ozone 37

P-wave 51
Pangaea 7
Pluto 53
Polaris 54, 55
phases of Moon 30
photosynthesis 38, 39
planet 38, 42, 52
plankton 16
precipitation 22

quarries 21
quartz 16, 23
quartzite 14

Richter scale 51
red giant 48
reservoirs 20
rock cycle 14
rotation of Earth 32

S-wave 51
San Andreas fault 51
Saturn 39, 52
Saturn rocket 42
Severn Tunnel 24

South Pole 28
Sun 28, 36, 38, 39, 40, 53
Surtsey 9
sandstone 14, 24, 44
satellite 40, 41
seasons 28
sedimentary rock 14, 16, 22, 23, 24, 44
solar system 38
star chart 54
strata 44
subduction 8, 50
supernova 48

tectonic plates 6, 8, 11
thunderstorms 33
tides 30
transport 14
trilobites 15

Universe 48, 54
Uranus 39

Venus 39, 52
volcanic island 7, 9
volcano 5, 6, 7, 14, 16, 46, 47

warm front 31
water 20
water cycle 22
weather 30, 31
weather map 31, 35
weathering 14
wells 20
white dwarf 48
wind 32, 33
wind speed 32